ENGLISH GRAMMAR FOR STUDENTS OF GERMAN

The Study Guide for Those Learning German

Second edition

Cecile Zorach
Franklin & Marshall College

Charlotte Melin
Williams College

The Olivia and Hill Press®

English Grammar series
edited by Jacqueline Morton

English Grammar for Students of French, 2nd ed.
English Grammar for Students of Spanish, 2nd ed.
English Grammar for Students of German, 2nd ed.
English Grammar for Students of Italian
English Grammar for Students of Latin
English Grammar for Students of Russian

Printed in the U.S.A.

Library of Congress Catalog Car Number: 80-82773

ISBN 0-934034-14-1

10 9 8 7 6 5 4 3 2 1

Contents

To the Student v

Introduction 1

What is a Noun? .4

What is Meant by Gender? 7

What is Meant by Number? 11

What are Articles? 14

What is Meant by Case? 18

What is a Verb? 26

What is a Subject? 30

What are Objects? 33

What is a Predicate Noun? 41

What is the Possessive? 43

What is a Pronoun? 47

What is a Personal Pronoun? 50

What are the Principal Parts of a Verb? 73

What is an Infinitive? 77

What is a Verb Conjugation? 79

What is Meant by Tense? 87

What is the Present Tense? 88

What is the Past Tense? 90

What are Auxiliary Verbs? 92

What is a Participle? 98

What are the Perfect Tenses? 109

What is the Future Tense? 114

What is Meant by Mood? 118

What is the Imperative? 119

What is the Subjunctive? 122

What is Meant by Direct and Indirect Discourse? 132

What is a Possessive Pronoun? 136

What is a Reflexive Pronoun? 139

What is a Reflexive Verb? 144

What is an Interrogative Pronoun? 147

What is a Relative Pronoun? 155

What is an Adjective? 169

What is a Descriptive Adjective? 170

What is Meant by Comparison of Adjectives? 175
What is a Possessive Adjective? 181
What is an Interrogative Adjective? 185
What is an Adverb? 189
What is a Preposition? 192
What are Prefixes and Suffixes? 198
What is Meant by Active and Passive Voice? 204
What is a Conjunction? 212
What are Sentences, Phrases, and Clauses? 216
Appendix--Selected Noun Gender Reference List 225
Answer Key 229
Index 235

To the Student

English Grammar for Students of German has been written to help you get the most out of your German textbook and to answer some of the questions you will have as you learn German.

BEFORE YOU DO YOUR GERMAN HOMEWORK

- Pick out the grammatical terms and concepts covered in the lesson you are about to study. You will find the terms you need to know in the table of contents or in the explanations in your textbook.
- Consult the index of **English Grammar for Students of German** to see where these topics are covered in this handbook.
- Read the relevant pages carefully, making sure that you understand the explanations and the examples.
- Do the **Practice** at the end of the chapters you have read.
- Compare your answers with the ones in the **Answer Key** at the end of this handbook.

Now you are ready to do your assignment for your German class.

STUDY TIPS

1. **Homework**—As you do the exercises, say the words aloud so that you practice seeing, saying, and hearing the words. Doing this will help you remember them.

2. **Memorization**—Memorization plays an important part in language learning. You will have to memorize vocabulary, verb conjugations, grammar rules, etc. Here are some steps to follow when you memorize new material:

   - Read the words or passage you must memorize several times aloud.
   - Write them down as you repeat them aloud to yourself.
   - Compare what you wrote with the original.

- Repeat the three steps above until you can easily write out what you have learned without any mistakes.
- Work at memorizing for only short periods of time. If you find you are not concentrating on the material, take a break or do a different part of your assignment.

3. **Vocabulary**—Use any trick or gimmick that will help you remember. Here are some that students have found useful:

   - Write each word on a different index card: German on one side, English on the other.
   - Use index cards of different colors to help you remember useful information. You might want to use different colors to help you remember the gender of nouns (i.e. blue for masculine, pink for feminine, yellow for neuter), or to identify different parts of speech (i.e. green for verbs, orange for adjectives).
   - Write the German word in the same color as the card.
   - When learning the words, flip through the cards looking at the German words. Say the word aloud, then think of the English word that corresponds. Flip the card to check your answer. Shuffle the deck often so that you see the words cold, i.e. so that they do not always appear in the same order. As you learn words, place those cards in a separate pile and concentrate on the ones you still need to learn.
   - Go through the cards working from English to German, saying the German word aloud for each card.
   - As you work on memorization, organize the cards in different groupings and spread them out in rows or other arrangements on your desk or floor. You might, for example, want to group together related vocabulary items (family members, hobbies, foods, etc.) or parts of speech that follow particular grammatical rules (i.e. strong verbs, weak verbs).
   - Remember that it is rare for there to be a perfect one-to-one correspondence between words in English and German. Make a note of important differences in meaning or usage on the cards.

4. **Rules**—Read the rules in your textbook and the handbook before looking at the examples. It's tempting to skip the rules and go to the examples, but if you do this, you may overlook important information about the grammar. Examples are merely illustrations; they do not show you how the rules apply in every case.

5. Make sure you understand each rule before you continue on to the next one. Language learning is like building a house, each brick is only as secure as its foundation.

6. Once you have mastered a new grammatical concept, make up simple examples on your own so that you can practice following the rules. Begin by modeling your sentences after the examples in your textbook. Later you will be able to express your own ideas accurately in writing and speaking.

7. **Class**—Take notes while you are in class. When your teacher gives you a new example, write it down so that you can analyze it for yourself later.

8. **Assignments**—Keep up with your assignments. You need daily practice and time to absorb new material when you are learning a language. Catching up is almost impossible because you can only memorize a certain amount of material at one time.

9. **Language laboratory**—It is better to listen to tapes for short periods at different times during the day than to try to do everything in one long sitting.

Viel Glück!
Jacqueline Morton

Introduction

When you learn a foreign language, in this case German, you need to look at each word in three ways:

1. The **meaning** of the word—You must connect an English word with a German word that has an equivalent meaning.

   Tree has basically the same meaning as the German word **Baum.**

Words with equivalent meanings are learned by memorizing **vocabulary** items. Sometimes two words are the same or very similar in both English and German. These words are called **cognates**. They are especially easy to learn.

GERMAN	ENGLISH
Haus	house
Garten	garden
Student	student
intelligent	intelligent

Sometimes knowing one German word will help you learn another.

   Knowing that **Kellner** is *waiter* should help you learn that **Kellnerin** is *waitress;* or knowing that **wohnen** means *to live* and that **Zimmer** means *room* should help you learn that **Wohnzimmer** means *living room.*

But usually there is little similiarity between words, and knowing one German word will not help you learn another. In general, you must learn each vocabularly item separately.

   Knowing that **Mann** means *man* will not help you learn that **Frau** means *woman.*

Even words that have the same basic meaning in English and German only rarely have identical meanings in all situations.

The German word **Mann** generally has the same meaning as the English word *man*, but it can also mean *husband*. The German word **Frau** usually means *woman*, but it can also mean a married woman, *Mrs.*, or even *Ms.*

In addition, there are times when words in combination take on a special meaning.

The German word **stehen** means to *stand;* **Schlange** basically means *snake*. But **Schlange stehen** means *to stand in line, to line up*.

An expression whose meaning as a whole (**Schlange stehen**) differs from the meaning of the individual words (**stehen** and **Schlange**) is called an **idiom**. You will need to pay special attention to these idiomatic expressions in order to recognize them and use them correctly.

2. The **classification** of a word—English and German words are classified in categories called **parts of speech**. We will consider eight different parts of speech used in German:

noun	article
pronoun	adverb
verb	preposition
adjective	conjunction

Each part of speech has its own rules for spelling and use. You must learn to identify each word as a part of speech so that you can choose the correct German equivalent and know what rules to apply.

Look at the word *that* in the following sentences:

    a. Have you read *that* newspaper?
    b. She said *that* she was busy.
    c. Here is the record *that* he bought.

The English word is the same in all three sentences, but in German three different words would be used and three different sets of rules would apply because each *that* is a different part of speech.[1]

3. The **use** of the word—A word must also be identified according to the role it plays in the sentence. Each word, whether English or German, has a specific role or **function** in the sentence. Determining the word's function will help you choose the correct German equivalent and know what rules apply.

Look at the word *her* in the following sentences:

    a. I don't know *her.*
    b. Have you told *her* your story?
    c. We know *her* father.

In English the word is the same, but in German the word for *her* will be different in each sentence because it has three different functions.[2]

As a student of German you must learn to recognize both the part of speech and the function of each word in a given sentence. This is essential because words in a German sentence have a great deal of influence on each other. Compare the following sentence in English and in German.

*The little blue **book** is on the big old table.*

Das kleine blaue **Buch** ist auf dem großen alten Tisch.

In English: In English, the only word that affects the form of another word in the sentence is *book*, which causes us to say *is*. If the word were *books*, we would have to say *are*.

---

[1] a. Adjective–see p. 169.
   b. Subordinating conjunction–see p. 212.
   c. Relative pronoun–see p. 155.
[2] a. Direct object–see p. 34.
   b. Indirect object–see p. 34.
   c. Possessive adjective–see p. 181.

In German: In German, the word for *book* (**Buch**) not only affects the word for *is* (**ist**), but also the spelling and pronunciation of the German words for *the* (**das**), *little* (**klein**), and *blue* (**blau**).

The words for *is on* (**ist auf**) and *table* (**Tisch**) affect the spelling and pronunciation of the equivalent words for *the* (**dem**), *big* (**groß**), and *old* (**alt**).

The only word not affected by the words surrounding it is the word for *on* (**auf**).

Since parts of speech and function are usually determined in the same way in English and German, this handbook will show you how to identify them in English. You will then learn to compare English and German constructions. This will give you a better understanding of the explanations in your German textbook.

What is a Noun?

A **noun** is a word that names something:

a person	friend, sister, brother, John, Mary, Professor Jones
a place	city, state, country, Austria, New York
a thing	desk, house, border, water, hand, Monday, environment
an animal	dog, bird, fish, Spot, Fluff
an event or activity	vacation, birth, death, jogging, growth
an idea or concept	truth, poverty, inertia, peace, fear, beauty

As you can see, a noun can name something tangible, i.e. that you can touch (*door, restaurant, cat,* etc.), or it can refer to something abstract, i.e., something you understand with your mind (*honor, love, justice, humor*).

In English: A noun that does not state the name of a specific person, place, thing, etc., is called a **common noun**. A common noun begins with a small letter, unless it is the first word of a sentence. All the words above that are not capitalized are common nouns. A noun that is the name of a specific person, place, thing, etc. is called a **proper noun**. A proper noun always begins with a capital letter. All the words above that are capitalized are proper nouns.

> Her name is Mary.
>
> common   proper
> noun   noun

A noun that is made up of two words is called a **compound noun**. A compound noun can be a common noun, such as *video game* and *ice cream,* or a proper noun, such as *Western Europe* and *North America.*

To help you learn to recognize nouns, here is a paragraph where the nouns are in ***bold italics***.

> The ***United States*** imports many useful ***items*** from German-speaking ***countries***. West German ***automobiles***, ranging from moderately-priced ***models*** to elegant ***cars***, enjoy great ***popularity*** with some ***Americans***. ***West Germany*** also supplies us with fine ***tools***, ***cameras***, and optical ***equipment***. Many ***Americans*** value their imported Swiss ***watches***. Nearly everyone in our ***country*** appreciates the ***taste*** of Swiss ***chocolate***. And some ***people*** here would feel lost in the ***winter*** without their ***pair*** of Austrian ***skis***.

In German: It is very easy to recognize nouns. German capitalizes all nouns, making no distinction between proper nouns and common nouns.

TERMS USED TO TALK ABOUT NOUNS

- A noun has gender; that is, it can be classified according to whether it is masculine, feminine, or neuter (see **What is Meant by Gender?**, p. 7).

- A noun has a number; that is, it can be described as being either singular or plural (see **What is Meant by Number?**, p. 11).

- A noun can have a variety of functions in a sentence; that is, it can be the subject of the sentence (see **What is a Subject?**, p. 30), a predicate noun (see **What is a Predicate Noun?**, p. 41), or an object (see **What are Objects?**, p. 33).

Practice

Circle the nouns in the following sentences:

1. The student asked the teacher a question.

2. Our textbook has a picture on the cover.

3. The curious children peered into the dark room.

4. Eric wants a new tape deck for his birthday.

5. The cows stood in the middle of a grassy field.

6. Actions speak louder than words.

7. My parents visited Berlin last year.

8. Honesty is the best policy.

9. The audience enjoyed her wit and candor.

10. The teacher's explanations were easy for the class to understand.

What is Meant by Gender?

Gender is the classification of a word as **masculine, feminine,** or **neuter**.

Gender plays only a small role in English; however, since it is at the very heart of the German language, let us see how we use gender in English and in German.

ENGLISH	GERMAN
pronouns	nouns
possessive adjectives	pronouns
	adjectives
	articles

Since each part of speech follows its own rules to indicate gender, you will find this discussed in the sections dealing with articles and with the various types of pronouns and adjectives. In this section we shall look only at the gender of nouns.

In English: Nouns themselves do not have gender, but sometimes when they stand for a person or animal, we treat them as if they had grammatical gender, based on their biological sex. If we replace a noun with *he* or *she*, we automatically use *he* for males and *she* for females. Nouns which name things that do not have a sex are replaced by *it*.

Nouns referring to males indicate the **masculine** gender.

The *boy* waved; *he* was tired, and I was glad to see *him*.
    | | |
    noun   masculine   masculine
    male

Nouns referring to females indicate the feminine gender.

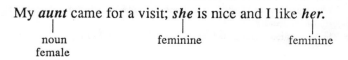

My *aunt* came for a visit; *she* is nice and I like *her*.
    | | |
    noun   feminine   feminine
    female

All other nouns do not indicate a gender; they are considered neuter.

There is a *tree* in front of the house. *It* is a maple.[1]
                 | |
               noun   neuter
               thing

In German: All nouns are either masculine, feminine, or neuter. This means that all objects, animals, events, and abstract ideas have a grammatical gender, as do the names of countries.

1. The gender of most German nouns cannot be explained or figured out. These nouns have a grammatical gender that is unrelated to biological sex. Here are some examples of English nouns whose equivalents in German have different genders.

NOUNS THAT HAVE *MASCULINE* EQUIVALENTS:	NOUNS THAT HAVE *FEMININE* EQUIVALENTS:	NOUNS THAT HAVE *NEUTER* EQUIVALENTS:
table	lamp	window
heaven	hope	girl
tree	plant	bread
month	season	year
state	Switzerland	Germany
beginning	reality	topic

You will have to memorize the grammatical gender of every German noun you learn. This gender is important not only for the noun itself, but also for the spelling and pronunciation of the words it influences.

---

[1] There are a few well-known exceptions, such as *ship*, which is referred to as *she*. It is custom, not logic, which decides.

The S/S United States sailed for Europe. *She* is a good ship.

2. It is easy to determine the gender of some nouns whose meaning is linked to biological sex.

> Males usually have masculine gender: Peter, boy, nephew, step-father.

> Females usually have feminine gender: Sarah, woman, sister, aunt.

> Often a German noun will have different forms when it refers to the different sexes. For example, the noun "student" has two equivalents, **Studentin** for females and **Student** for males (see **Appendix,** p. 225).

A number of German nouns, however, have a grammatical gender that does not correspond to the biological sex of the persons or animals they name. The words for *baby, child,* and *girl* are all neuter because they refer to young or small beings. You will want to pay extra attention to such words because it is easy to forget that they have a special grammatical gender in German.

ENDINGS INDICATING GENDER

Gender can sometimes be determined by looking at the ending of a German noun. The list on p. 225 shows you noun endings which often occur in masculine, feminine, and neuter nouns. You will find it helpful to familiarize yourself with these endings as you learn individual nouns in your German course.

Practice

I. You will have to consult a dictionary to find the gender of most German nouns.
- Look at the examples below.
- Use biological sex to determine the gender of the living beings listed here.
- Write "?" next to the nouns whose gender you would have to look up in the dictionary.

GENDER IN GERMAN

1. clock   _____

2. mother   _____

3. son   _____

4. pear   _____

5. radio   _____

II. By consulting the list on p. 225, determine the gender of the following German words.

GENDER IN GERMAN

1. Lehrer   _____

2. Brötchen   _____

3. Freundin   _____

4. Sonntag   _____

5. Buchhandlung   _____

What is Meant by Number?

Number in the grammatical sense means that a word is singular or plural. When a word refers to one person or thing, it is said to be **singular**; when it refers to more than one, it is **plural**.

In German, more parts of speech indicate number than in English, and there are more spelling and pronunciation changes in German that show number as well. Parts of speech that indicate number:

ENGLISH	GERMAN
nouns	nouns
verbs	verbs
pronouns	pronouns
only demonstrative adjectives	adjectives
	articles

Since each part of speech follows its own rules to indicate number, you will find number discussed in the sections dealing with articles, the various types of adjectives and pronouns, as well as in all sections on verbs and their tenses. In this section we will look at number in nouns only.

In English: We form the plural of nouns in several ways:

- by adding *-s* or *-es* to a singular noun

book	books
kiss	kisses

- by making a spelling change

man	men
leaf	leaves
child	children

A plural noun is usually spelled and pronounced differently from the singular.[1]

Some nouns, called **collective nouns,** refer to a group of persons or things, but the noun itself is considered singular.

> A soccer *team* has eleven players.
> The *family* is well.
> The *crowd* was under control.

In German: There are several ways of making a singular noun plural. German plurals are less predictable than English ones; they are more like the *man/men* or *child/children* nouns in English.

Buch	→ Bücher	book	→ books
Wagen	→ Wagen	car	→ cars
Vater	→ Väter	father	→ fathers
Gast	→ Gäste	guest	→ guests
Frau	→ Frauen	woman	→ women

Notice that German can use an **umlaut** (¨) to form plural nouns. This changes both the spelling of the word and its pronunciation. As you learn new nouns in German, you should memorize each noun's gender and its singular and plural forms. Consult the list on p. 225 for some hints about how different genders form their plural.

Note: Nouns do not change gender when they become plural.

---

[1] A few nouns have only one form for both the singular and the plural, i.e., sheep → sheep.

Practice

I. Here is a list of English nouns.
  • Circle the word if it is plural.

1. pencils

2. suitcase

3. business

4. feet

5. group

II. The following is a list of German nouns in their singular and plural form.
  • Compare the singular form of each noun with its plural form.
  • Under the PLURAL column, circle the parts of the word that indicate the plural form.

SINGULAR	PLURAL
1. Wort	Wörter
2. Stuhl	Stühle
3. Kind	Kinder
4. Student	Studenten
5. Auto	Autos

What are Articles?

An **article** is a word placed before a noun to show whether the noun refers to a particular person, animal, place, thing, event, or idea, or whether the noun refers to an unspecified person, animal, place, thing, event, or idea.

In English: Let us look at the two types of articles.

1. **Definite article**—The is used before a noun when we are speaking about a particular person, place, animal, thing, event, or idea.

   > I saw *the* boy you met yesterday.
   > a particular boy

   > I ate *the* apple you gave me.
   > a particular apple

   The definite article remains *the* when the noun it precedes becomes plural.

   > I saw *the boys* you met yesterday.
   > I ate *the apples* you gave me.

2. **Indefinite articles**—A or an is used before a noun when we are not speaking about a particular person, animal, place, thing, event, or idea.

   A is used before a word beginning with a consonant.

   > I saw *a* boy in the street.
   > not a particular boy

An is used before a word beginning with a vowel.[1]

I ate *an* apple.

not a particular apple

The indefinite article is used only with a singular noun. When the noun becomes plural, we omit it or replace it with the word **some.**

I saw boys in the street.
I saw *some* boys in the street.

I ate apples.
I ate *some* apples.

In German: You will have to pay much more attention to German articles than to their English counterparts. Although German has the same two types of articles as English, definite and indefinite, these articles have different forms because they must match the noun to which they belong. This "matching" is called **agreement** (we say that "the article agrees with the noun"). To choose the correct form of the article, you must know the following information about the noun to which it belongs: gender, number, and case (see **What is Meant by Case?**, p. 18).

To introduce you to articles, we will give you only the basic form of the article as you will find it in your textbook vocabulary list or in the dictionary. In the chapter **What is Meant by Case?**, p. 18, you will see how these forms change according to the article's function in a sentence.

1. Definite articles

Der indicates that the noun is masculine singular.

der Baum   *the tree*

---

[1] Vowels are the letters *a, e, i, o,* and *u;* consonants are the other letters of the alphabet.

Die indicates that the noun is feminine singular.

    die Tür   *the door*

Das indicates that the noun is neuter singular.

    das Haus   *the house*

Die is also the plural definite article. In the plural, the gender of the noun is not important because the article **die** is used with masculine, feminine, and neuter plural nouns.

    die Türen   *the doors*

Since the same definite article **die** is used for plural nouns and for feminine singular nouns, you will have to rely on other indicators to determine the number of the noun. The most common indicator is the form of the noun itself: is it the singular form or the plural form?

    die Tür   **die** Türen
        singular   plural
    die = feminine

    the door   *the doors*

You will discover other indicators of number as you learn more German (see **What is Meant by Case?**, p. 18, and **What is a Verb Conjugation?**, p. 79).

2. Indefinite articles

As in English, the indefinite article is used only with a singular noun in German.

Ein indicates that the noun is masculine or neuter.

    ein Baum   *a tree*
        masculine

ein H<u>au</u>s   *a house*
|
neuter

Eine indicates that the noun is feminine.

eine T<u>ü</u>r   *a door*
|
feminine

Your German textbook will discuss the different forms of the definite and indefinite articles in greater detail.

Practice

I. Here is a list of German nouns as they appear in a dictionary. The DICTIONARY ENTRY shows you whether the noun is masculine (*m.*), feminine (*f.*), or neuter (*n.*).

- Write the German definite article for each noun in the space provided.

	ARTICLE	DICTIONARY ENTRY
1.	_____	Bett, *n.*
2.	_____	Woche, *f.*
3.	_____	Kugelschreiber, *m.*
4.	_____	Uhr, *f.*
5.	_____	Heft, *n.*

II. The following is a list of German nouns preceded by definite and indefinite articles, together with their English equivalents.
 • Write the appropriate English article in the space provided.

1. die Straße   _____   street

2. ein Bleistift   _____   pencil

3. der Zug   _____   train

4. ein Zimmer   _____   room

5. das Wetter   _____   weather

What is Meant by Case?

Case indicates how certain words function within a sentence. The case of a word is shown by the particular form of the word itself, by the form of the words that accompany it, or by the position of the word in the sentence.

Case is very important in German because it affects the form of several parts of speech. Let us look at how case is indicated in English and German:

ENGLISH	GERMAN
word order	nouns
form of pronouns	form of pronouns
	form of adjectives
	form of articles

In English: The order of the words in the sentence signals the function of the nouns and gives meaning to the whole sentence. We easily recognize the difference in meaning between the following two sentences purely on the basis of word order. The nouns themselves remain the same even though they serve different functions in the two sentences:

> The girl gives the teacher the apple.
>
> > Here *the girl* is giving,
> > and *the teacher* is receiving.
>
> The teacher gives the girl the apple.
>
> > Here *the teacher* is giving,
> > and *the girl* is receiving.

If we begin moving the words around, we can make up nonsense sentences:

> The apple is giving the teacher the girl.
> The girl is giving the apple the teacher.

These sentences show how we completely change the meaning of an English sentence by changing the position (and therefore the function and case) of the nouns.

CASE OF ENGLISH PRONOUNS

We are most aware of case in English when we use pronouns. (See **What is a Personal Pronoun?**, p. 50.) In the two examples below, it is not only word order but also the form, i.e., the case, of the pronoun that affects the sentence's meaning:

> *I* know *them*.
> *They* know *me*.

We cannot say, "I know *they*" or "They know *I*" because the forms "they" and "I" cannot be used as objects of a verb (see **What are Objects?**, p. 33). If you learn to recognize the different cases of pronouns in English you will find it easier to understand the German case system.

English pronouns have three cases:

1. **Nominative**—It is used when a pronoun is a subject or a predicate nominative. Predicate nominatives are discussed in a separate section on predicate nouns. (See **What is a Subject?**, p. 30 and **What is a Predicate Noun?**, p. 41.)

> *She* and *I* went to the movies.
> subjects =
> nominative case

> *We* enjoyed the film.
> subject =
> nominative case

> It was *he* who did the deed.
> predicate nominative =
> nominative case

2. **Objective**—It is used when a pronoun is a direct object, an indirect object, or an object of a preposition (see **What are Objects?**, p. 33).

> *They* invited both *him* and *me*.
> subject =   direct objects =
> nominative case   objective case

> *They* sent *us* a note.
> subject =   indirect object =
> nominative   objective

> *We* asked about *them*.
> subject =   object of preposition =
> nominative   objective

In these examples, the form of the pronoun changes because the pronoun has different functions in the sentences. *We* and *us* refer to the same people, but *we* can only function as the subject of a sentence. (You can't say "*Us* went to the movies.") *They* and *them* refer to the same people, but only *they* can function as the subject of a sentence. (You can't say "*Them* asked about me.") *They* and *them* are different cases of the same pronoun, as are *we* and *us, she* and *her, he* and *him,* and *I* and *me.*

3. **Possessive**—It is used when a pronoun shows ownership. The possessive pronoun can function as subject, predicate noun, direct object, indirect object, or object of a preposition.

> Is this book *yours?*
> |
>   possessive pronoun =
>   predicate noun

> Kit called her parents, but I wrote *mine* a letter.
> |
>   possessive pronoun =
>   indirect object

> Mary has finished her test, but John is still working on *his.*
> |
> possessive pronoun =
> object of preposition

The possessive case is discussed in a separate section (see **What is a Possessive Pronoun?**, p. 136).

In German: Word order does not indicate the function of nouns within a sentence. Instead, the function of a noun in a sentence is indicated by either the form of the word itself or the form of the definite or indefinite article. These different forms indicate case. As long as the nouns are put in their proper cases, the words in the sentence can be moved around in a variety of ways without changing the essential meaning of the sentence.

Look at the many ways the following sentence can be expressed in German using the nominative case and two objective cases (accusative and dative) to indicate function:

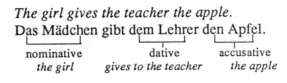

The girl gives the teacher the apple.
Das Mädchen gibt dem Lehrer den Apfel.

nominative	dative	accusative
the girl	*gives to the teacher*	*the apple*

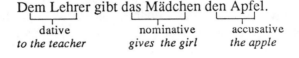

Dem Lehrer gibt das Mädchen den Apfel.

dative	nominative	accusative
to the teacher	*gives the girl*	*the apple*

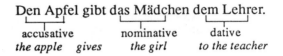

Den Apfel gibt das Mädchen dem Lehrer.

accusative	nominative	dative
the apple gives	*the girl*	*to the teacher*

With the different case endings on the articles (**das, dem, den,** all meaning "the"), all three of these sentences show that *the girl* (**das Mädchen**—nominative in all three sentences) is doing the giving and *the teacher* (**dem Lehrer**—dative in all three sentences) is doing the receiving. The different word order in all three sentences simply shows what part of the sentence the speaker wants to emphasize.

CASE OF GERMAN NOUNS

German has four different cases for nouns:

1. the nominative
2. the accusative
3. the dative
4. the genitive

The complete set of case forms for any noun (indicated primarily by the endings given to the accompanying article) is called the noun's **declension**. When you have memorized these forms, you are able to "decline" that noun. Let us look at a set of noun declensions in German:

	MASCULINE	SINGULAR FEMININE	NEUTER	PLURAL
NOMINATIVE	**der** Apfel	**die** Tür	**das** Kind	**die** Bücher
ACCUSATIVE	**den** Apfel	**die** Tür	**das** Kind	**die** Bücher
DATIVE	**dem** Apfel	**der** Tür	**dem** Kind	**den** Büchern
GENITIVE	**des** Apfels	**der** Tür	**des** Kindes	**der** Bücher

As you can see, case affects the form of the noun in the masculine and neuter genitive singular and in the plural dative.[1] The definite article also reflects case and changes its form depending on how the noun functions in a sentence.

Here is a list of the different functions a word can have in a sentence and the case corresponding to each function:

The **nominative case** is used for the subject of a sentence and for predicate nouns. (See **What is a Subject?**, p. 30 and **What is a Predicate Noun?**, p. 41.)

The **accusative case** is used for most direct objects. (See **What are Objects?**, p. 33.)

The **dative case** is used for indirect objects and for the object of a few verbs that you will have to memorize.

The **genitive case** is used to show possession or close relation. (See **What is the Possessive?**, p. 43.)

---

[1] A small group of nouns, called weak nouns, have different forms to indicate case. Your textbook will explain their declension together with other exceptions.

The **accusative, dative,** and occasionally the **genitive** are used as the objects of prepositions. (See **What is a Preposition?**, p. 192.)

To show you how a change in case leads to a change in meaning, let us take the sentence used above, "The girl gives the teacher the apple," and change it to mean "The teacher gives the girl the apple," simply by changing the case of the nouns in German. Notice that the definite articles in these two sentences indicate the different functions of the nouns.

The girl gives the teacher the apple.

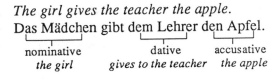

nominative	dative	accusative
the girl	*gives to the teacher*	*the apple*

The teacher gives the girl the apple.

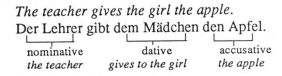

nominative	dative	accusative
the teacher	*gives to the girl*	*the apple*

To choose the appropriate case for each noun in the second German sentence, you need to go through a series of steps:

The teacher gives the girl the apple.

1. Identify the gender and number of each noun.

teacher:	**Der Lehrer** is masculine singular.
girl:	**Das Mädchen** is neuter singular.
apple:	**Der Apfel** is masculine singular.

2. Determine how each noun functions in the sentence.

teacher	=	subject
girl	=	indirect object
apple	=	direct object

3. Determine what case in German corresponds to the function you have identified in step 2.

teacher = subject   ⟶ nominative case
girl   = indirect object ⟶ dative case
apple = direct object   ⟶ accusative case

4. Choose the proper form from those which you have memorized.

Der Lehrer gibt dem Mädchen den Apfel.

masculine	neuter	masculine
singular	singular	singular
nominative	dative	accusative

Your textbook will show you the different case forms for the definite and indefinite articles and explain how to use them. As you learn more German, you will discover other ways in which case affects the form of nouns, pronouns, and adjectives (see **What is a Personal Pronoun?**, p. 50, and **What is an Adjective?**, p. 169). Understanding case will help you master these new points of grammar.

Practice

I. In the following English sentences, circle the words that will be affected by case in a German sentence.

1. The children ran after the ball.

2. When the cat is away, the mice will play.

3. A car pulled out of the drive.

4. An insider leaked the story to the press.

5. The end of the movie was a surprise.

II. Here is a list of the various functions in a German sentence and the corresponding cases.
- Fill in the missing information.

FUNCTION   CASE

subject   _____

_____   accusative

indirect object   _____

_____   genitive

_____   accusative, dative, or genitive

What is a Verb?

A **verb** is a word that expresses "the action" of the sentence. Here the word "action" is used in its broadest sense and is not necessarily limited to physical action.

In English: Verbs can express many different types of action:

a physical activity	to run, to walk, to hit, to sit
a mental activity	to dream, to think, to believe, to hope
a condition	to be, to become, to seem

Many verbs, however, do not fall neatly into one of these categories. They are still verbs because they represent "the action" of the sentence.

The book *costs* $5.00.
|
to cost

I *have* a cold.
|
to have

To help you learn to recognize verbs, here is a paragraph where the verbs are in *bold italics:*

> The three students *entered* the restaurant, *selected* a table, *hung* up their coats and *sat* down. They *looked* at the menu and *asked* the waitress what she *recommended*. She *suggested* the daily special, roast chicken. It *was* not expensive. They *chose* a bottle of white wine and *ordered* a salad. The service *was* slow, but the food *tasted* excellent. Good cooking, they *decided, takes* time. They *ate* pastry for dessert and *finished* the meal with coffee.

The verb is one of the most important words of a sentence; you cannot express a complete thought (i.e., write a **complete sentence**) without a verb. It is important for you to learn to identify verbs because the function of many words in a sentence depends on their relationship to the verb. For example, the subject of a sentence performs the action of the verb, and the object receives the action of the verb (see **What is a Subject?**, p. 30 and **What are Objects?**, p. 33).

Transitive and Intransitive Verbs

There are two types of verbs in both English and German: transitive and intransitive.

A **transitive verb** is a verb that takes a direct object. (See **What are Objects?**, p. 33.) It is indicated by the abbreviation *v.t.* (verb transitive) in dictionaries.

The boy *threw* the ball.
　　　　|
　　transitive |
　　　　　direct object

She *lost* her job.
　　| |
transitive |
　　　direct object

An **intransitive verb** is a verb that cannot take a direct object. It is indicated by the abbreviation *v.i.* (verb intransitive) in dictionaries.

Laura *arrives* today.
　　| |
intransitive |
　　　　adverb

Brian *is sleeping*.
└─────┬─────┘
intransitive

Many verbs can be used both transitively and intransitively, but in every case the above distinction remains true: transitive usage permits a direct object, and intransitive usage does not.

The students *speak* German.
　　　| |
　transitive |
　　　　direct object

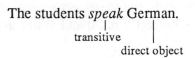

Actions *speak* louder than words.
　　| └─────┬─────┘
intransitive |
　　　　adverbial phrase

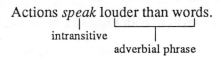

In German: Verbs are identified the same way that they are in English. However, some verbs that are transitive in English are intransitive in German, while other verbs that are intransitive in English are transitive in German. You will find several examples of how verbs function differently in German and in English in the sections **What are Objects?**, p. 33 and **What is a Reflexive Verb?**, p. 144.

- The verb form which is the name of the verb is called an infinitive: *to eat, to sleep, to drink* (see **What is an Infinitive?**, p. 77).

- A verb is conjugated or changes in form to agree with its subject: *I do, she does* (see **What is a Verb Conjugation?**, p. 79).

- A verb indicates tense, that is, the time (present, past, or future) of the action: *I am, I was, I will be* (see **What is Meant by Tense?**, p. 87).

- A verb shows voice, that is, the relation between the subject and the action of the verb (see **What is Meant by Active and Passive Voice?**, p. 204).

- A verb shows moods, that is, the speaker's attitude toward what he or she is saying (see **What is Meant by Mood?**, p. 118).

- A verb may also be used to form a participle (see **What is a Participle?**, p. 98).

Practice

Circle the verbs in the following sentences.

1. The students eat their lunch at school.

2. Robin and Jeff met at the library.

3. We stayed home because we expected a phone call.

4. Rachel took a bath, finished her novel, and went to bed.

5. Sam felt better after he talked to his friends.

What is a Subject?

The **subject** of a sentence is the person or thing that performs the action.[1]

In English: To find the subject of a sentence, look for the verb first (see **What is a Verb?**, p. 26); then ask, *who?* or *what?* before the verb. The answer will be the subject.

>   Peter studies German.
>
> > *Who* studies German?
> > Answer: Peter.
> > *Peter* is the subject.
> > (Note that the subject is singular. It refers to one person.)
>
>   Did the packages come yesterday?
>
> > *What* came yesterday?
> > Answer: the packages.
> > *The packages* is the subject.
> > (Note that the subject is plural. It refers to more than one thing.)

Train yourself always to ask this question to find the subject. Never assume a word is the subject because it comes first in the sentence. Subjects can be located in several different places, as you can see in the following examples (the **subject** is in boldface and the *verb* italicized):

>   After running 26 miles, **Ann** *was* very tired.
>   Standing at the top of the stairs *was* a tall **man**.

Some sentences have more than one main verb; you must find the subject of each verb.

---

[1] The subject performs the action in an active sentence, but is acted upon in a passive sentence (see **What is Meant by Active and Passive Voice?**, p. 204).

> The *boys were doing* the cooking while **Mary** *was setting* the table.
>
> > *Boys* is the plural subject of *were doing*.
> > *Mary* is the singular subject of *was setting*.

In English and in German it is very important to find the subject of each verb and to make sure that the subject and verb agree. You must choose the form of the verb which goes with the subject (see **What is a Verb Conjugation?**, p. 79).

In German: It is particularly important that you recognize the subject of a sentence so that you put it in the proper case (see **What is meant by Case?**, p. 18). The subject of a German sentence is in the nominative case.

> **Das Kind** spielt allein.
> nominative
> 3rd person singular neuter
>
> *The child is playing alone.*

> **Wir** kommen spät.
> nominative
> 1st person plural
>
> *We are coming late.*

> **Petra** und **Franz** arbeiten heute.
> nominative
> 3rd person plural
>
> *Petra and Franz are working today.*

Practice

Find the subjects in the following English sentences.
- Next to Q write the question you need to ask to find the subject.
- Next to A write the answer to the question you asked.

1. The bus leaves in fifteen minutes.

   Q:_____

   A:_____

2. When the game was over, everyone went home.

   Q:_____

   A:_____

3. Emily checked the books out of the library.

   Q:_____

   A:_____

4. Suddenly Stefan could see the solution.

   Q:_____

   A:_____

5. My friends and I took a boat ride down the Rhine.

   Q:_____

   A:_____

What are Objects?

Most sentences consist, at the very least, of a subject and a verb:

> Children play.
> Work stopped.

The subject of the sentence is usually a noun (see **What is a Noun?**, p. 4) or a pronoun (see **What is a Personal Pronoun?**, p. 50). Many sentences contain other nouns or pronouns that are related to the action of the verb or to a preposition. We call these nouns or pronouns **objects**.

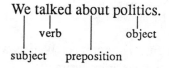

> Ingrid wants an answer.
> subject   verb   object

> She sent us a letter.
> subject verb object   object

> We talked about politics.
> subject verb preposition object

There are three types of objects:

1. direct object
2. indirect object
3. object of a preposition

1. Direct Object and 2. Indirect Object of a Verb

In English: Let us see how we can identify these two types of objects of the verb.

1. **Direct object**—This is a noun or pronoun that receives the action of the verb or shows the result of that action directly, without a preposition.[1] It answers the question *what?* or *whom?* asked after the verb.

> Paula reads *the book.*
>
> > Paula reads *what?* The book.
> > The book is the direct object.

> They are inviting *Paula* and *her sister.*
>
> > They are inviting whom? Paula and her sister.
> > *Paula* and *her sister* are the two direct objects.

Never assume that a word that comes right after a verb is the direct object. It must answer the question *what?* or *whom?*

> John writes well.
>
> > John writes *what?* No answer.
> > John writes *whom?* No answer.

There is no direct object in this sentence. *Well* is an adverb; it answers the question "*How* does John write?"

2. **Indirect object**—This is a noun or pronoun that receives the action of the verb, or shows the result of that action indirectly. It explains "to whom," "to what," "for whom," or "for what" the action of the verb is done. It answers the question *to whom/for whom?* or *to what/for what?* asked after the verb.

---

[1]   In this section, we will consider only active sentences (see What is **Meant by Active and Passive Voice?**, p. 204).

John writes *his brother.*

> John writes *to whom?* To his brother.
> *His brother* is the indirect object.

Susan did *me* a favor.

> Susan did a favor *for whom?* For me.
> *Me* is the indirect object.

In German: Objects are divided into categories depending on their case, mainly accusative and dative. An object will never be in the nominative, and you will rarely encounter an object in the genitive.

1. **Direct object**—Most English direct objects are expressed by the accusative case in German.

> *Paula reads the book.*
>
> > Paula reads *what?* The book.
> > *The book* is the direct object.
>
> Paula liest **das Buch.**
> subject   neuter singular
>   direct object = accusative

> *They are inviting **Paula and her sister.***
>
> > They are inviting *who(m)?* Paula and her sister.
> > *Paula* and *her sister* are the direct objects.
>
> Sie laden **Paula** und **ihre Schwester** ein.
> subject   direct objects = accusative

A few common German verbs require a dative object even though their English equivalents have direct objects. Your German textbook will tell you about these verbs, and you will need to memorize them. Here are two examples:

*They thank **the policeman.***

>They thank *who(m)?* The policeman.
>*The policeman* is the direct object.

Sie danken **dem Polizisten.**
| |
subject dative object

>The verb **danken** (*to thank*) requires a dative object.

*We are helping **you.***

>We are helping *who(m)?* You.
>*You* is the direct object.

Wir helfen **dir.**
| |
subject dative object

>The verb **helfen** (*to help*) requires a dative object.

2. **Indirect object**—Most English indirect objects are expressed by the dative case in German.

*John writes **his brother.***

>John writes *to whom?* His brother.
>*His brother* is the indirect object.

John schreibt **seinem Bruder.**
| |
subject dative object

*Susan did **me** a favor.*

>Susan did a favor *for whom?* Me.
>*Me* is the indirect object.

Susan tat **mir** einen Gefallen.
| | |
subject dative accusative
          object   object

As you can see from the example above, many verbs in English and in German have both direct and indirect objects. Let us look at another example to see how to recognize the two types of objects:

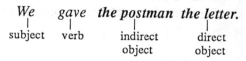

$$
\begin{array}{llll}
\textit{We} & \textit{gave} & \textit{the postman} & \textit{the letter.} \\
\text{subject} & \text{verb} & \text{indirect} & \text{direct} \\
& & \text{object} & \text{object}
\end{array}
$$

> We gave *what?* The letter.
> *The letter* is the direct object.

> We gave the letter *to whom?* To the postman.
> *The postman* is the indirect object.

$$
\begin{array}{llll}
\text{Wir} & \text{gaben} & \textbf{dem Briefträger} & \textbf{den Brief.} \\
\text{subject} & \text{verb} & \text{dative} & \text{accusative} \\
& & \text{indirect} & \text{direct} \\
& & \text{object} & \text{object}
\end{array}
$$

Often the indirect object in an English sentence is expressed using the preposition *to* or *for*. We could say, for example, "We gave the letter to the postman." Notice that *the postman* is still the indirect object.

3. OBJECT OF A PREPOSITION

In English: The noun or pronoun which follows a preposition is called the **object of the preposition** (see **What is a Preposition?**, p. 192). It answers the question *what?* or *whom?* asked after the preposition.

> The book is *in the desk.*

> The book is *in what?* In the desk.
> *The desk* is the object of the preposition *in*.

> John is working *for Gretchen.*

> John is working *for whom?* For Gretchen.
> *Gretchen* is the object of the preposition *for*.

In German: Objects of a preposition are as easy to identify as they are in English. German prepositions, however, have objects in particular cases, usually accusative or dative, and sometimes genitive (see **What is Meant by a Preposition?**, p. 192). As you memorize prepositions, you will need to learn which case each preposition takes. For example, here are three different prepositions, each requiring a different case:

um diese Stadt

accusative with **um**

around this city

von solchen Büchern

dative with **von**

about such books

wegen des Sturmes

genitive with **wegen**

on account of the storm

OBJECTS IN ENGLISH AND GERMAN

As a student of German you must watch out for the following pitfalls:

1. An English verb that requires a preposition before its object may have a German equivalent that requires simply an accusative.

    *She is looking for **her coat**.*

    She is looking *for what?* Her coat.
    Her coat is the object of the preposition *for*.

    Sie sucht **ihren Mantel.**

    accusative object

    The verb **suchen** is the equivalent of *to look for* and takes an accusative object.

2. The preposition that follows a German verb may be different from the preposition that follows an English verb.

> *He is waiting for his friend.*
> Er wartet **auf** seinen Freund.
>
literally, *on*

> *I am asking you for advice.*
> Ich bitte dich **um** Rat.
>
literally, *about*

Always remember that German is a separate language with structures different from English; then you will avoid the error of translating word-for-word from English into German. Your German textbook will introduce phrases like **warten auf** + accusative object (*to wait for*) and **bitten um** + accusative object (*to ask for*). Make sure you learn the verb together with the preposition and its case so that you can use the entire pattern correctly.

Practice

The following sentences contain different types of objects.
- Next to Q write the question you need to ask to find the object.
- Next to A write the answer to the question you just asked.
- In the column to the right, identify the kind of object you found by circling the appropriate letters: direct object (DO), indirect object (IO), or object of a preposition (OP).

1. The computer lost my homework.

Q: _____ DO IO OP

A: _____

2. She borrowed the car.

    Q:_____ DO IO OP

    A: _____

3. Are you worried about the test?

    Q:_____ DO IO OP

    A: _____

4. He sent his friend a postcard.

    Q:_____ DO IO OP

    A:_____

    Q:_____ DO IO OP

    A:_____

5. My parents paid for the books with a credit card.

    Q:_____ DO IO OP

    A:_____

    Q:_____ DO IO OP

    A:_____

What is a Predicate Noun?

A **predicate noun** is a noun in a sentence that refers to the same thing as the subject of the sentence.

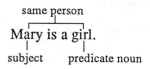

A predicate noun is connected to the subject by a **linking verb**, a verb which *links* interchangeable elements.

In English: The most common linking verbs in English are *to be* and *to become*. Although these verbs often have a noun after them in the sentence, this noun does not receive the action of the verb and is not a direct object (see **What are Objects?**, p. 33); instead, it is called a predicate noun.

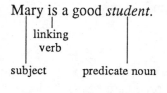

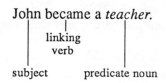

In German: Predicate nouns are in the nominative case (see **What is Meant by Case?**, p. 18) because they point to the subject, which is also in the nominative case.

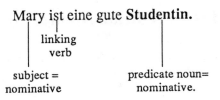

Mary is a good student.

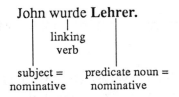

John became a teacher.

You should learn to recognize linking verbs like **sein** (*to be*), **werden** (*to become*), and **scheinen** (*to appear*), which often have a predicate noun following them.

Practice

The following sentences contain predicate nouns.
- Circle the predicate noun in each example.
- Draw an arrow from the the subject to the predicate noun to which it refers.

1. The letter was really good news.

2. Carol became a doctor.

3. They are tourists.

4. Dan became an accomplished musician.

5. The swimming pool is our favorite place in the summer.

What is the Possessive?

The **possessive** is used to show that one noun possesses or owns another noun, or that the two nouns have a similar, close relation to each other.

In English: You can show possession in one of two ways:

1. with an *apostrophe*

- by adding apostrophe + *s* to a singular possessor

> Inge's mother
> Goethe's poetry
> the child's ball
> the professor's book

- by adding an apostrophe to a plural possessor

> the girls' father
> the boys' school

2. with the word *of*

- by adding *of* before a proper noun possessor

> the poetry *of* Goethe
> the mother *of* Inge

- by adding *of a (an)* or *of the* before a singular or plural common noun

> the branches *of a* tree
> the shape *of an* egg
> the book *of the* professor
> the teacher *of the* students

In German: There are also two ways of showing possession:

1. By using the genitive case. The genitive case is formed as follows:

- most names add **-s**

    Inges Mutter
    Inge's mother
    | |
    possessor possessed

    Goethes Dichtung
    Goethe's poetry

With the names of people, the possessor comes before the thing possessed, just as in English. Note, however, that German does not use an apostrophe, except with proper nouns ending in -s or -z.

- most masculine and neuter singular nouns of one syllable add **-es**. The accompanying articles likewise end in **-s**:

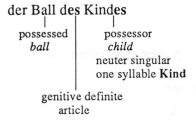

    der Ball des Kindes
        | | |
    possessed | possessor
      ball | child
               | neuter singular
               | one syllable **Kind**
               |
          genitive definite
              article

    the child's ball

- most masculine and neuter singular nouns of more than one syllable add **-s**

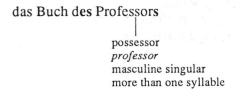

    das Buch des Professors
                    |
                possessor
                professor
                masculine singular
                more than one syllable

    the professor's book

With nouns that are not proper nouns, the possessor follows the thing possessed. The German structure parallels the English *of the* structure (see 2 above).

• feminine and plural nouns have no special genitive ending themselves. To indicate possession, you add **-er** to the preceding article or adjectives.

> der Mantel der **Frau**
> |
>   feminine singular
>
> *the woman's coat*

> der Vater der **Mädchen**
> |
>   neuter plural
>
> *the girls' father*

> Kisten alter **Bücher**
> |
>   neuter plural
>
> *boxes of old books*

Your German textbook will explain the genitive in greater detail and will point out a few irregularities that occur.

2. By using **von** + the dative case. This structure is used with proper and common nouns and corresponds to using *of* in English to express possession.

> die Mutter **von** Inge
> *the mother of Inge*

> die Dichtung **von** Goethe
> *the poetry of Goethe*

der Motor **vom** Auto

| von + dem |

the motor of the car

der Vater **von den** Mädchen
the father of the girls

In general, **von** + the dative is used to express possession in colloquial German while the genitive case is used in writing and in formal language.

Practice

The following are possessive constructions using the apostrophe.
- Write the alternate English structure using the word *of*.
- Underline the possessor in your new construction.

1. the car's motor

_____

2. a test's results

_____

3. the year's end

_____

4. two cities' tale

_____

5. Schiller's works

_____

What is a Pronoun?

A **pronoun** is a word used in place of one or more nouns. Therefore it may stand for a person, place, thing, or idea.

For example, instead of repeating the proper noun "Karen" in the following two sentences, it sounds more natural to use a pronoun in the second sentence:

> *Karen* likes to sing.   *Karen* practices every day.
> *Karen* likes to sing.   *She* practices every day.

Generally a pronoun is used to refer to something (or someone) that has already been mentioned. The word that the pronoun replaces is called the **antecedent** of the pronoun. In the example above, the pronoun *she* refers to the proper noun *Karen*. *Karen* is the antecedent of the pronoun *she*.

In English: There are different types of pronouns, each serving a different function and following different rules. The list below presents the most important types and refers you to the section where they are discussed in detail.

Personal pronouns—These pronouns refer to different persons (1ˢᵗ, 2ⁿᵈ, or 3ʳᵈ) and they change their form according to the function they have in a sentence (see p. 50). The personal pronouns include:

Subject pronouns—These pronouns are used as the subject of a verb (see p. 50).

> *I* go.   *They* read.   *He* runs.

Object pronouns—These pronouns can be used as:

* a direct object (see p. 55)

> Jane loves *him*.
> Mark saw *them* at the theater.

- an indirect object (see p. 55)

> The boy wrote *me* the letter.
> Petra gave *us* the book.

- an object of a preposition (see p. 62)

> Robert is going to the movies with *us*.
> Don't step on *it;* walk around *it*.

Reflexive pronouns—These pronouns refer back to the subject of the sentence (see p. 139).

> I cut *myself*.
> She spoke about *herself*.

Interrogative pronouns—These pronouns are used in questions (see p. 147).

> *Who* is that?
> *What* do you want?

Possessive pronouns—These pronouns are used to show possession (see p. 136).

> Whose book is that? *Mine*.
> *Yours* is on the table.

Relative pronouns—These pronouns are used to introduce relative subordinate clauses (see p. 155).

> The man *who* came is very nice.
> Meg, *whom* you met, wants to study in Berlin.

In German: Pronouns are identified in the same way as in English. The most important difference is that German pronouns use more case forms than English pronouns (see **What is Meant by Case?**, p. 18). German pronouns must also agree in gender and number with the nouns they replace; that is, they must correspond in gender and number to their antecedents.

Practice

The following sentences contain different types of pronouns.
- Circle the pronouns.
- Draw an arrow from the pronoun to its antecedent(s).

1. Did Brooke phone? Yes, she called a few minutes ago.

2. Molly and Stan were out. They had a lot of errands to run.

3. If the paper is not next to the chair, look under it.

4. Jim baked the cake himself.

5. Has Brad met Helga yet? Yes, Brad already knows her.

What is a Personal Pronoun?

Both in English and in German, we use **personal pronouns** to refer to different persons or things:

I and *we*	used by the person(s) speaking; called 1st person pronouns
you	used for the person(s) spoken to; called 2nd person pronouns
he, she, it, *they*	used for the person(s) or thing(s) spoken about; called 3rd person pronouns

These personal pronouns (except *you*) clearly indicate number; that is, they show whether one person or more than one is involved. *We* and *they* are plural pronouns; *I* and *she* are singular.

In both German and English, a personal pronoun has different forms to show its function in a sentence; these forms are called **case forms** (see **What is Meant by Case?**, p. 18). For example, *we* and *us* are different cases of the first-person plural pronoun. Personal pronouns can function as subjects, objects, and objects of prepositions. These functions are discussed below.

A. PERSONAL PRONOUNS AS SUBJECTS

In the following examples a personal pronoun is used as the subject:

> *They* ran, but *I* walked.
>
> Who ran? Answer: They.
> *They* is the subject of the verb *ran*.
>
> Who walked? Answer: I.
> *I* is the subject of the verb *walked*.

Let us compare the subject pronouns in English and German. In both languages, the form of the pronoun used for the subject is called the **nominative form** (see **What is Meant by Case?**, p. 18). Although the case system is much more developed in German than in English, understanding the cases of pronouns in English can help you understand how cases work in German.

	ENGLISH nominative case	GERMAN nominative case
SINGULAR		
1st PERSON the person speaking	*I*	**ich**
2nd PERSON the person spoken to	*you*	**du/Sie**
3rd PERSON the person or thing spoken about	*he* *she* *it*	**er** **sie** **er/sie/es**
PLURAL		
1st PERSON the person speaking + others *Mary* and *I* speak German. we	*we*	**wir**
2nd PERSON the persons being spoken to *Mary* and *you* speak German. you plural	*you*	**ihr/Sie**
3rd PERSON the persons or objects spoken about *Mary* and *John* speak German. they	*they*	**sie**

As you can see from the chart above, two subject pronouns in English have more than one equivalent in German: *you* and *it*. Let us look more closely at them so that you will know how to choose the correct word.

YOU—THE FAMILIAR AND FORMAL FORMS

In English: *You* is always used to address another person or persons. We use the same pronoun *you* to speak to a pet or to the President of the United States.

> What are *you* chewing on, *you* silly dog?
> Mr. President, are *you* concerned about acid rain?

Likewise, there is no difference between *you* in the singular and *you* in the plural. For example, if dozens of people were standing in a room and you asked, "Are *you* coming with me?" the *you* could refer to one person or to many.

In German: There are two sets of pronouns for *you:*

1. Familiar *you*—**du** or **ihr**

   The familiar forms of *you* are used with members of one's family, friends, children, and pets. In general, you use the familiar forms with persons you call by a first name.

   du = familiar singular *you*
             It addresses one person.

> Inge, bist **du** jetzt endlich fertig?
> *Inge, are **you** finished now?*

> Hans, was machst **du?**
> *Hans, what are **you** doing?*

ihr = familiar plural *you*
It addresses more than one person
to whom you say **du.**

Maria und Inge, was macht **ihr**?
Maria and Inge, what are you doing?

Hans und Peter, kommt **ihr** mit?
Hans and Peter, are you coming along?

2. Formal *you*—**Sie**

The formal form of *you* is used to address one or more persons
you do not know very well. It is the same form (**Sie**) in both the
singular and the plural, that is, if you are addressing one or more
than one person.

Herr Braun, kommen **Sie** mit?
Mr. Braun, are you coming along?

Herr und Frau Braun, kommen **Sie** mit?
Mr. and Mrs. Braun, are you coming along?

NOTE: If you are uncertain whether you should use the familiar or
the formal you, use the formal form, unless you are speaking to a
child or an animal.

IT—**er, sie,** or **es**

In English: Whenever you refer to one thing or idea, you use the
pronoun *it*.

Where is the pencil? *It* is lying on the table.
How was the trip? *It* was nice.
Where is the book? *It* is on the table.

In German: The singular pronoun you use depends on the gender of the noun it replaces (see **What is Meant by Gender?**, p. 7). The pronoun must correspond in gender to its antecedent. Thus it will be either masculine, feminine, or neuter.

To choose the correct form of *it*, you must:

1. Find the noun *it* replaces, the antecedent.
2. Determine the gender of the antecedent in German.

Below you will find an example of each gender:

- masculine antecedent

    *Where is the pencil? **It** is lying on the table.*

    Noun *it* replaces: the pencil
    Gender: **Der Bleistift** (*pencil*) is masculine.

    Wo ist der Bleistift? **Er** liegt auf dem Tisch.

    masculine singular
    subject pronoun = nominative

- feminine antecedent

    *How was the trip? **It** was nice.*

    Noun *it* replaces: trip
    Gender: **Die Reise** (*trip*) is feminine.

    Wie war die Reise? **Sie** war sehr schön.

    feminine singular
    subject pronoun = nominative

- neuter antecedent

    *Where is the book? **It** is on the table.*

    Noun *it* replaces: the book
    Gender: **Das Buch** (*book*) is neuter.

    Wo ist das Buch? **Es** ist auf dem Tisch.

    neuter singular
    subject pronoun = nominative

B. PERSONAL PRONOUNS AS OBJECTS

In the following examples a personal pronoun is used as an object.

> She saw *us*.
>
>> She saw *whom*? Us.
>> *Us* is the direct object of *saw*.

> They wrote *me*.
>
>> They wrote to *whom*? Me.
>> *Me* is the indirect object of *wrote*.

In English: Most pronouns that occur as objects in a sentence are different in form from the ones used as subjects. When pronouns are used as the direct or indirect object or as the object of a preposition in English they are said to be in the **objective case** (see **What are Objects?**, p. 33).

> *He* and *I* work for the newspaper.
>
>> subject
>> nominative case

> They invited *him* and *me*.
>
>> direct object
>> objective case

> I lent *them* my car.
>
>> indirect object
>> objective case

> They are coming with *you* and *her*.
>
>> object of a preposition
>> objective case

Compare the nominative and objective cases of English pronouns:

	NOMINATIVE	OBJECTIVE
SINGULAR		
1st PERSON	I	me
2nd PERSON	you	you
3rd PERSON	he	him
	she	her
	it	it
PLURAL		
1st PERSON	we	us
2nd PERSON	you	you
3rd PERSON	they	them

The form of the object pronoun is the same regardless of whether the pronoun is used as a direct object, an indirect object, or an object of a preposition.

In German: Instead of a single objective case, there are two cases of pronouns which are used for direct and indirect objects: the accusative and the dative. The objects of prepositions may be accusative or dative. (A few prepositions take the genitive case, but because this rarely occurs with personal pronouns, we will not discuss this matter here.) The use of these different cases corresponds to the use of the same cases for nouns (see **What is Meant by Case?**, p. 18). The chart below lists each English objective pronoun and the two corresponding forms, accusative and dative, in German:

	OBJECTIVE	ACCUSATIVE		DATIVE
SINGULAR				
1st PERSON	me	mich		mir
2nd PERSON	you	dich *(familiar)*		dir
		Sie *(formal)*		Ihnen
	him	ihn	*(masculine)*	ihm
3rd PERSON	her	sie	*(feminine)*	ihr
	it	es	*(neuter)*	ihm
PLURAL				
1st PERSON	us	uns		uns
2nd PERSON	you	euch *(familiar)*		euch
		Sie *(formal)*		Ihnen
3rd PERSON	them	sie		ihnen

In general, once you have learned the functions of the German cases for nouns, you will have no difficulty knowing the case of pronouns, since the cases are the same. Two object pronouns in English, however, have more than one equivalent in German: you and it. Let us look more closely at them so that you can learn how to choose the correct form.

You—THE FAMILIAR AND FORMAL FORMS

1. Familiar *you*—**dich/dir** or **euch**

The familiar *you* has its accusative and dative forms for the singular and plural.

- familiar singular (**du** = nominative)

    dich   =   accusative
    dir   =   dative

> *We see you, Anna.*
> Wir sehen **dich**, Anna.
>> familiar singular
>> direct object = accusative

> *We are helping you, Anna.*
> Wir helfen **dir**, Anna.
>> familiar singular
>> dative object of **helfen**

- familiar plural (**ihr** = nominative)

> **euch** = accusative
> **euch** = dative

> *We see you, Effi and Franz.*
> Wir sehen **euch**, Effi und Franz.
>> familiar plural
>> direct object = accusative

> *We are helping you, Effi and Franz.*
> Wir helfen **euch**, Effi und Franz.
>> familiar plural
>> dative object of **helfen**

2. Formal *you*—**Sie** or **Ihnen**

The formal form of *you* (**Sie** = nominative) also has its own accusative and dative forms. The same forms are used when addressing one or more persons.

Sie = accusative
Ihnen = dative

> *We will see you tomorrow, Mrs. Erb.*
> Wir sehen **Sie** morgen, Frau Erb.
>> formal
>> direct object = accusative

Prof. and Mrs. Mayer, we will certainly call you.
Prof. und Frau Mayer, wir rufen Sie bestimmt an.
         |
       formal
    direct object = accusative

We're glad to help you, Dr. Fried.
Wir helfen **Ihnen** gern, Dr. Fried.
    |
   formal
 dative object of **helfen**

HIM—**ihn** or **ihm**

The German equivalent for the English pronoun *him* has two forms: accusative and dative. To choose the correct one, you will have to determine the function of the pronoun *him* in the sentence.

- **ihn** = accusative

  *Did you see the man? Yes, I saw **him**.*

  > Noun *him* replaces: the man
  > Gender: **Der Mann** (*the man*) is masculine.
  > Function: direct object of *see* (sehen)
  > Case: accusative

  Hast du **den Mann** gesehen? Ja, ich habe **ihn** gesehen.
     └──┬──┘ |
     masculine   masculine singular
     singular   accusative object

- **ihm** = dative

  *Who helps the man? We are helping **him**.*

  > Noun *him* replaces: the man
  > Gender: **Der Mann** (*the man*) is masculine.
  > Function: object of *help* (**helfen** takes a dative object)
  > Case: dative

  Wer hilft **dem Mann**? Wir helfen **ihm**.
     └──┬──┘ |
     masculine   masculine singular
     singular   dative object

HER—sie or ihr

The German equivalent for the English pronoun *her* has two forms: accusative and dative. To choose the correct one, you will have to determine the function of the pronoun *her* in the sentence.

- **sie** = accusative

    Do you see the woman? Yes, I see her.

    > Noun *her* replaces: the woman
    > Gender: **Die Frau** (*the woman*) is feminine.
    > Function: direct object of *see* (**sehen**)
    > Case: accusative

    Hast du **die Frau** gesehen? Ja, ich habe **sie** gesehen.

    feminine   feminine singular
    singular   accusative object

- **ihr** = dative

    Who helps the woman? We are helping her.

    > Noun *her* replaces: the woman
    > Gender: **Die Frau** (*the woman*) is feminine.
    > Function: object of *help* (**helfen** takes a dative object)
    > Case: dative

    Wer hilft **der Frau**? Wir helfen **ihr.**

    feminine singular   feminine singular
                             dative object

IT—ihn/ihm, sie/ihr, es/ihm

The English pronoun *it* used as an object has six German equivalents: feminine, masculine, and neuter, each with an accusative and dative form. You will have to determine the gender of the noun that the pronoun *it* replaces and the function of *it* in the sentence. To choose the correct form, follow these steps:

1. Find the noun *it* replaces, the antecedent.
2. Determine the gender of the antecedent in German.
3. Determine the function of *it* in the sentence.

4. Choose the case that corresponds to the function found in step 3.
5. Select the proper form depending on the gender (step 2) and case (step 4).

Let us look at some examples:

- masculine antecedent ——→ **ihn** = accusative; **ihm** = dative

    Did you see the film? Yes, I saw it.

    Noun *it* replaces: the film
    Gender: **Der Film** (*the film*) is masculine.
    Function: direct object of *see* (**sehen**)
    Case: accusative

    Hast du **den Film** gesehen? Ja, ich habe **ihn** gesehen.
    ⎣—⊤—⎦ |
    masculine   masculine singular
    singular   accusative object

- feminine antecedent ——→ **sie** = accusative; **ihr** = dative

    Are you reading the newspaper? Yes, I am reading it.

    Noun *it* replaces: the newspaper
    Gender: **Die Zeitung** (*the newspaper*) is feminine.
    Function: direct object of *read* (**lesen**)
    Case: accusative

    Lesen Sie **die Zeitung**? Ja, ich lese **sie.**
    ⎣—⊤—⎦ |
    feminine   feminine singular
    singular   accusative object

- neuter antecedent ——→ **es** = accusative, **ihm** = dative

    Do you understand the book? Yes, I understand it.

    Noun *it* replaces: the book
    Gender: **Das Buch** is neuter.
    Function: direct object of *understand* (**verstehen**)
    Case: accusative

    Verstehen Sie **das Buch**? Ja, ich verstehe **es.**
    ⎣—⊤—⎦ |
    neuter   neuter singular
    singular   accusative object

Since the pronoun you select depends on the gender of the German noun replaced, you will also use **es** and **ihm** when you replace neuter nouns that refer to people. In English you refer to these people using *her* or *him*.

> *Who helps the child? We are helping **her/him**.*
>
>> Noun replaced: the child
>> Gender: **Das Kind** is neuter.
>> Function: object of *help* (**helfen** takes a dative object)
>> Case: dative

> Wer hilft **dem Kind**? Wir helfen **ihm**.

                   neuter   neuter singular
                 singular   dative object

C. PERSONAL PRONOUNS AS OBJECTS OF PREPOSITIONS

In English: We can replace any noun object of a preposition with a pronoun object. The pronoun can replace a person or a thing.

- a person

> John talked about *his sister*. John talked about *her*.

              noun object of   pronoun object of
            preposition *about*   preposition *about*

- a thing

> Beth talked about *her work*. Beth talked about *it*.

              noun object of   pronoun object of
            preposition *about*   preposition *about*

In German: The objects of prepositions in German are in the accusative, dative, or genitive case (see **What is a Preposition?**, p. 192). Normally we replace the noun object of a preposition with a pronoun object only if the noun refers to a person. A different construction is used when the pronoun refers to a thing or idea. Let us look at the two types of constructions.

• a person

When the pronoun object of a preposition refers to a person (or an animal), you will follow the steps you have already learned to choose the appropriate personal pronoun:

1. Find the noun replaced, the antecedent.
2. Determine the gender of the antecedent in German.
3. Identify the case required by the preposition used in the sentence.
4. Select the appropriate pronoun form from the chart on p. 57.

Below are examples showing how to analyze sentences that have a pronoun referring to a person as the object of a preposition.

> *Molly is buying something for **her brother.***
> Molly kauft etwas für **ihren Bruder.**
>
> > Antecedent: brother
> > Gender: **Der Bruder** (*brother*) is masculine.
> > Case: **für** takes an accusative object
> > Selection: **ihn**
>
> *Molly is buying something for **him.***
> Molly kauft etwas für **ihn.**

> *John talked about **his sister.***
> John sprach von **seiner Schwester.**
>
> > Antecedent: sister
> > Gender: **Die Schwester** (*sister*) is feminine.
> > Case: **von** takes a dative object
> > Selection: **ihr**
>
> *John talked about **her.***
> John sprach von **ihr.**

- a thing or idea

Normally a pronoun cannot be the object of a preposition when you refer to a thing or an idea. When you encounter the English construction preposition + *it* or preposition + *them*, you will need to use a special German construction called a **da-compound** or a **pronominal adverb**. This construction takes the place of a preposition + a pronoun. It is formed by adding the prefix **da-** to the preposition (**dar-** if the preposition begins with a vowel). Let us look at some examples:

Don't think about the work.
Denken Sie nicht **an die Arbeit.**

        preposition   noun (a thing)
                object of preposition an

Don't think about it.
Denken Sie nicht **daran!**

    da-construction:
    da + r + preposition an

Beth talked about her courses.
Beth sprach **von ihren Kursen.**

    preposition   noun (a thing)
             object of preposition von

Beth talked about them.
Beth sprach **davon.**

    da-construction:
    da + preposition von

Your German textbook will discuss this construction and its use in greater detail.

SUMMARY

Below is a flow chart of the steps you must follow to find the German equivalents for English personal pronouns. It is important that you do the steps in sequence, because each step depends on the previous one.

S	=	subject in a German sentence
DO	=	direct object in a German sentence
IO	=	indirect object in a German sentence
DV	=	dative object required by the German verb
OP	=	object of a preposition

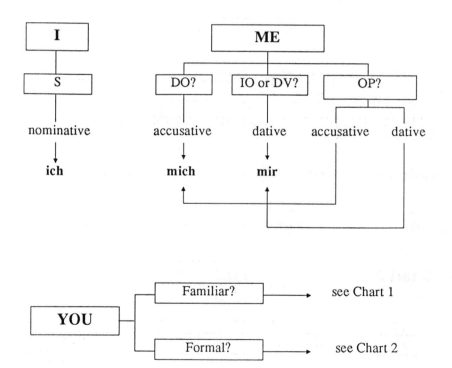

Chart 1

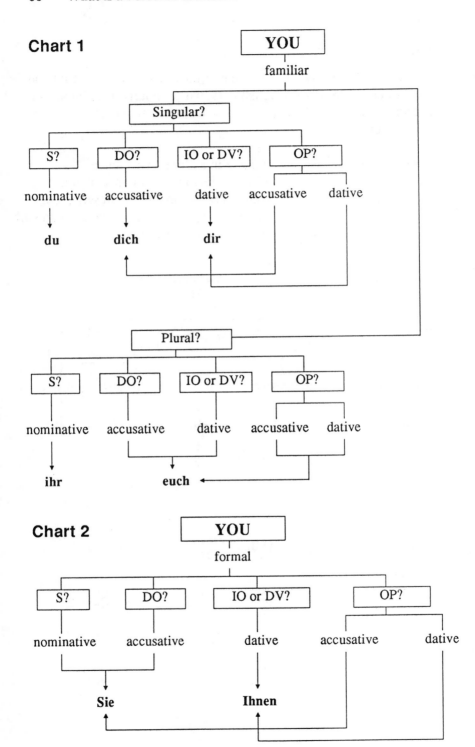

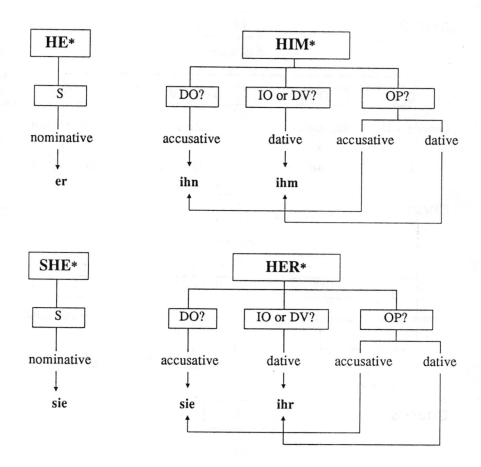

* Remember that German nouns referring to persons may be masculine, feminine, or neuter, in gender. If the antecedent is a neuter noun, i.e., **das Kind** (*the child*), you must use the neuter third person personal pronoun, **es** (nominative and accusative) or **ihm** (dative).

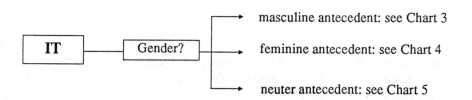

Chart 3

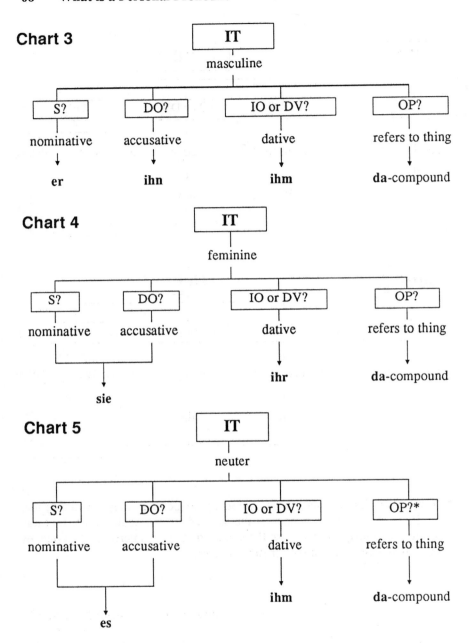

* Remember that if the antecedent is a neuter noun that refers to a person, i.e., **das Kind** (*the child*), the pronoun object of the preposition will be **es** (accusative) or **ihm** (dative).

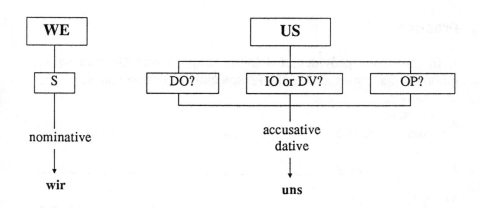

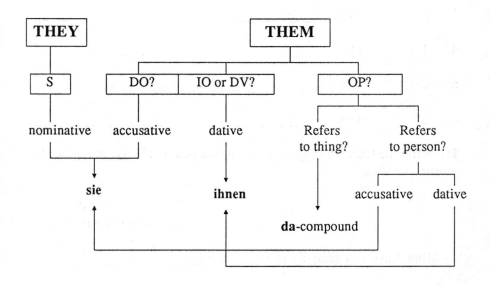

Practice

I. In the space provided, fill in the English and German subject pronouns that correspond to the PERSON and NUMBER indicated:

	PERSON	SUBJECT NUMBER	ENGLISH	GERMAN
1.	1st	sing.	_____	_____
2.	3rd	pl.	_____	_____
3.	2nd	sing.	_____	_____
4.	1st	pl.	_____	_____
5.	2nd	pl.	_____	_____
6.	3rd	sing.	_____	_____

II. Write the German subject pronoun that you would use to replace the words in italics:

GERMAN
SUBJECT PRONOUN

1. Mom, have *you* seen my jacket?   _____

2. *Cathy and I* are going out.   _____

3. Children, *you* must come inside.   _____

4. *My brother and sister* went
   to the movies.   _____

5. Dr. Clark, what do *you* think?   _____

III. Decide which pronouns you would use to replace the subjects of these sentences.
- Write the English subject pronoun in the first column.
- Use the translations given to fill in the corresponding German nominative pronoun in the second column.

	ENGLISH	GERMAN

1. *The window* is open.
   = das Fenster

   _____ _____

2. *The street* was deserted.
   = die Straße

   _____ _____

3. *The cake* tastes great.
   = der Kuchen

   _____ _____

IV. These English sentences contain prepositions and their objects written in italics.
- Circle italicized nouns referring to persons.
- Underline italicized nouns referring to things.
- Check the type of construction you must use in German.

	PREPOSITION + PERSONAL PRONOUN	*da*-COMPOUND

1. We're waiting *for Greg*.

   _____ _____

2. Thank you *for the present!*

   _____ _____

3. I wrote *to Emily.*

   _____ _____

4. We're looking forward *to the vacation.*

   _____ _____

5. Everyone talks *about the weather.*

   _____ _____

V. The German sentences below give examples of pronouns in different cases.
- Using the chart on p. 57, supply the information requested about the pronouns in italics.

1. Ich glaube *dir.*

    Person: _____

    Number: _____

    Case: _____

2. Das Bild gefällt *ihr.*

    Person: _____

    Number: _____

    Case: _____

    Gender: _____

3. Sie besuchen *mich.*

    Person: _____

    Number: _____

    Case: _____

4. Wir sahen *ihn* oft.

    Person: _____

    Number: _____

Case: _____

Gender: _____

5. Kommst du zu *mir?*

Person: _____

Number: _____

Case: _____

What are the Principal Parts of a Verb?

The **principal parts** of a verb are the forms we need to create all the different tenses. (See **What is Meant by Tense?**, p. 87.)

In English: The principal parts of an English verb are the infinitive, past tense, and past participle forms. (See **What is an Infinitive?**, p. 77, **What is the Past Tense?**, p. 90, and **What is a Participle?**, p. 98.) If you know these forms, you can apply rules to form all the other tenses of the verb.

For example, in order to form the six main tenses of the verb *to eat,* we need to know the parts *eat* (the form used in the infinitive), *ate* (simple past), and *eaten* (past participle):

PRESENT	I *eat*
PRESENT PERFECT	I have *eaten*
PAST	I *ate*
PAST PERFECT	I had *eaten*
FUTURE	I will *eat*
FUTURE PERFECT	I will have *eaten*

English verbs fall into two categories depending on how they form their principal parts:

1. **Regular verbs** form their past tense and past participle predictably by simply adding -*ed,* -*d,* or -*t* to the base of the infinitive.

INFINITIVE	PAST TENSE	PAST PARTICIPLE
to walk	walked	walked
to seem	seemed	seemed
to burn	burned	burned
	or burnt	or burnt

Since the past tense and the past participle of regular verbs are identical, these verbs have only two distinct principal parts, the infinitive and the simple past form.

2. **Irregular verbs** have unpredictable principal parts. As we grow up, we learn these forms simply by hearing them, although some of them give us difficulty and require extra effort to master. Examples of verbs with irregular principal parts include the following:

INFINITIVE	PAST TENSE	PAST PARTICIPLE
to sing	sang	sung
to draw	drew	drawn
to hit	hit	hit
to lie	lay	lain
to ride	rode	ridden

In German: The principal parts are essentially the same as in English: the infinitive, the past tense, and the past participle. For some verbs a fourth principal part (discussed below) is also important.

German verbs fall into two categories[1] depending on how they form their principal parts:

---

[1] A small group of irregular verbs falls between these two categories. Your German textbook will show you how to form the principal parts of these verbs.

1. **Weak verbs** resemble English regular verbs in that they form their principal parts predictably, using the stem of the verb. The stem is the main part of the verb, the part that gives us the verb's meaning (to find the stem, see p. 84).

Past tense—They form their past tense by adding a **t-** (or if the verb stem ends in **-d** or **-t,** by adding **-et-**) to the stem of the infinitive and then adding the endings for the different persons.

Past participle—They form their past participle by adding the prefix **ge-** and the suffix **-t** or **-et** to the stem of the verb.

INFINITIVE	PAST TENSE (3rd per. sing.)	PAST PARTICIPLE
machen	machte	gemacht
arbeiten	arbeitete	gearbeitet
glauben	glaubte	geglaubt

2. **Strong verbs,** like English irregular verbs, have unpredictable principal parts. You will simply have to memorize them as new vocabulary.

Past tense and past participle—The vowel of the infinitive stem may change in the past and in the past participle.

Past participle—The past participle ends in **-en,** or, rarely, in **-n.** There is no additional **-t** in either the past tense or the past participle as there is in the weak verbs.

INFINITIVE	PAST TENSE (3rd per. sing.)	PAST PARTICIPLE
finden	fand	gefunden
kommen	kam	gekommen
verlieren	verlor	verloren
singen	sang	gesungen
tun	tat	getan

Present tense—Some strong verbs also have a change in the stem vowel in the 2nd and 3rd person singular of the present tense. In these cases you will need to know a fourth principal part:

INFINITIVE	PRESENT (3rd per. sing.)	PAST TENSE	PAST PARTICIPLE
laufen	er läuft	lief	gelaufen
lesen	liest	las	gelesen
schlafen	schläft	schlief	geschlafen
nehmen	nimmt	nahm	genommen

Only by memorizing the principal parts of these verbs can you conjugate them properly in all their tenses.

Practice

I. The list below gives the principal parts of some regular and irregular verbs in English.
 • Fill in the missing principal parts of these verbs.

1. to open   opened   _____

2. to come   _____   come

3. to wash   _____   washed

4. to drink   drank   _____

5. _____   fell   fallen

II. Here are the principal parts of some German verbs.
  • Check the appropriate column to indicate whether they are weak or strong.

	WEAK	STRONG
1. kaufen—kaufte—(hat) gekauft		
2. beginnen–begann–(hat) begonnen		
3. liegen—lag—(hat) gelegen		
4. fragen—fragte—(hat) gefragt		
5. sitzen—saß—(hat) gesessen		

What is an Infinitive?

An **infinitive** is the form of the verb found in the dictionary as the main entry.

In English: The infinitive is used together with a main verb, that is a conjugated verb, to form various types of sentences. (See **What is a Verb Conjugation?**, p. 79.) When using an infinitive in a sentence, we often combine *to* + the dictionary form of the verb *to be, to walk, to think, to enjoy*:

> *To learn is* challenging.
> infinitive   main verb

> It *is* important *to be* on time.
> main verb   infinitive

Bob and Mary *want to play* tennis.
main verb   infinitive

It *has started to rain.*
main verb   infinitive

After some verbs, such as *must* and *let*, we use the **dictionary form** of the verb, i.e. the infinitive, without the *to*.

Matt *must do* his homework.
main verb   infinitive

The parents *let* the children *open* the presents.
main verb   infinitive

In German: The infinitive ends with the letters **-n** or **-en**. It is used in a variety of ways. There will generally be another conjugated verb with it that serves as the main verb in the sentence.

Bob wants to play tennis.
Bob will Tennis **spielen.**
conjugated verb   infinitive

Mary doesn't have to work.
Mary braucht nicht **zu arbeiten.**
conjugated verb   infinitive

Practice

The following English sentences contain verbs written in italics.
- Under what word would you look up these verbs in the dictionary?
- Write this infinitive form in the space provided.

1. We *taught* them everything they know.   _____

2. I *am* tired today.   _____

3. They *had* a good time.   _____

4. She *leaves* next week for Konstanz.   _____

5. He *swam* every day in the summer.   _____

What is a Verb Conjugation?

A **verb conjugation** is a list of the six possible forms of the verb for a particular tense. For each tense, there is one verb form for each of the six persons used as the subject of the verb. (See **What is a Personal Pronoun?**, p. 50.)

In English: Most verbs change very little. Let us look at the various forms the verb *to sing* takes when each of the six possible pronouns is the subject.[1]

---

[1] In this section we will talk only about the present tense (see **What is the Present Tense?**, p. 88).

SINGULAR

1st PERSON	*I sing* with the music.
2nd PERSON	*You sing* with the music.

3rd PERSON
- *He sings* with the music.
- *She sings* with the music.
- *It sings* with the music.

PLURAL

1st PERSON	*We sing* with the music.
2nd PERSON	*You sing* with the music.
3rd PERSON	*They sing* with the music.

Because English verbs change so little, you do not need to "conjugate verbs." It is much simpler to say that verbs add an -s in the 3rd person singular. The verb *to be* has the most forms: I *am*, you *are*, he *is*.

In German: German verbs have many more forms than English verbs. Fortunately, the conjugations are quite predictable for most verbs, once you have learned a few simple rules.

A. SUBJECT

Let us look at the same verb *to sing* that we conjugated in English, paying special attention now to the personal subject pronoun (see p. 50):

SINGULAR

1st PERSON	**ich** singe
2nd PERSON FAMILIAR	**du** singst

3rd PERSON
- **er** singt
- **sie** singt
- **es** singt

PLURAL

1st PERSON	**wir** singen
2nd PERSON FAMILIAR	**ihr** singt
2nd PERSON FORMAL	
(singular & plural)	**Sie** singen
3rd PERSON	**sie** singen

1st person singular—The *I form* of the verb (the **ich** form) is used whenever the person speaking is the doer of the action.

> *I sing softly.*
> **Ich singe** leise.

2nd person singular—The *you familiar singular form* of the verb (the **du** form) is used whenever the person spoken to (with whom you are on familiar terms, see p. 52) is the doer of the action.

> *Molly, **you sing** well.*
> Molly, **du singst** gut.

3rd person singular—The 3rd person singular form of the verb (the **er, sie, es** form) is used when the person, thing, or idea spoken about is the doer of the action. The 3rd person singular form is used with:

1. the third person singular masculine pronoun **er** (*he* or *it*), feminine pronoun **sie** (*she* or *it*), and the neuter pronoun **es** (*it*):

> **Er singt** schön.   *He sings beautifully.*
> **Sie singt** schön.   *She sings beautifully.*
> **Es singt** schön.   *It sings beautifully.*

2. one proper name:

> **Anna singt** gut.   *Anna sings well.*

3. a singular noun:

Der Vogel **singt.**	*The bird sings.*
Die Geige **singt.**	*The violin sings.*
Das Kind **singt.**	*The child sings.*

1ˢᵗ person plural—The *we form* of the verb (the **wir** form) is used whenever *I* (the speaker) is one of the doers of the action; that is, whenever the speaker is included in a plural or multiple subject.

Peter, Paul, Mary and I sing well.

In English: *we* form

Peter, Paul, Mary und ich **singen** gut.

In German: **wir** form

In this sentence, the subject, *Peter, Paul, Mary and I,* could be replaced by the pronoun *we*; thus in German you must use the **wir** form (1ˢᵗ person plural) of the verb.

2ⁿᵈ person plural familiar—The *you plural familiar form* of the verb (the **ihr** form)is used whenever you are addressing more than one person to whom you say **du.**

Molly, do you sing too?	*Win, do you sing too?*
Molly, **singst du** auch?	Win, **singst du** auch?

Molly and Win, do you sing also?
Molly und Win, **ihr singt** auch?

2ⁿᵈ person formal, singular and plural—The *formal you form* of the verb (the **Sie** form), singular and plural, is used whenever you are addressing one or more persons to whom you say Sie.

Mrs. Smith, are you coming along with us?
Frau Smith, **kommen Sie** mit?

In German: Sie form

*Mr. and Mrs. Smith, **are you coming** along with us?*
Herr und Frau Smith, **kommen Sie** mit?

In German: Sie form

3rd person plural—The *they form* of the verb (the **sie** form) is used whenever you are speaking about two or more persons or things that do not include either the speaker or the person spoken to.

*The children **sing** in the choir.*
Die Kinder **singen** im Chor.

In German: sie form

*Paul and Mary **sing** a duet.*
Paul und Mary **singen** ein Duett.

In German: sie form

(Compare: Paul, Mary, and I *sing*. . .)

In German: **wir** form

*The glasses and plates **are** on the table.*
Die Gläser und Teller **sind** auf dem Tisch.

In German: sie form

In the three sentences above, the subject could be replaced by the pronoun *they;* thus in German you must use the **sie** form, the 3rd person plural of the verb.

B. VERB FORM

Let us look again at the verb *to sing*, paying special attention to its different forms.

ich	singe
du	singst
er	singt
sie	singt
es	singt
wir	singen
ihr	singt
sie	singen
Sie	singen

A German verb is composed of two parts:

1. **the stem,** which we obtain by dropping the final -en from the infinitive (or with a few verbs like **tun** and **ändern** by dropping the final -n).

INFINITIVE	STEM
singen	sing-
machen	mach-
kommen	komm-

2. **the personal endings,** which change for each person, with some overlap.

As you can see in the verb **singen** conjugated above, the endings for the present tense are -e, -st, -t, -en, -t, -en.

To use a verb correctly in a sentence you must:

- Find the verb stem by removing the infinitive ending.

brauchen	brauch-
infinitive ending	stem

- Add the ending that agrees with the subject.

  *I **need** help.*
  |
  subject *I* = **ich** form

  Ich **brauche** Hilfe.
  |
  verb stem **brauch-** + ending **-e**

  *We **need** help too.*
  |
  subject *we* = **wir** form

  Wir **brauchen** auch Hilfe.
  |
  verb stem **brauch-** + ending **-en**

Some verb stems require slight adjustments in the endings. In addition, many of the so-called strong verbs change their stem in the **du** and **er/sie/es** form of the present tense. (See **What are the Principal Parts of a Verb?**, p. 73.) Finally, a very few German verbs are irregular in the present tense, that is, they do not follow a predictable pattern. Your German textbook will give you the conjugations of these irregular verbs.

Practice

I. Below is a list of German verbs in the infinitive form.
  - Draw a box around the stem of these verbs.

1. denken

2. rennen

3. arbeiten

4. wandern

5. reisen

II. This is the German verb **bringen** conjugated in present tense.
- Circle the personal endings.

> ich bringe
>
> du bringst
>
> er/sie/es bringt
>
> wir bringen
>
> ihr bringt
>
> sie/Sie bringen

III. Conjugate the verb **gehen.**
- Find its stem.
- Next add the endings that agree with each person and write the six conjugated forms.

ich _____

du _____

er/sie/es _____

wir _____

ihr _____

sie/Sie _____

IV. The following sentences in English have different types of subjects.
- Underline the subject(s) of the sentence.
- Write the pronoun form you would use in German to replace each subject.

                                                                    FORM

1. Matt and I wanted to play tennis.   _____

2. Have you heard anything yet, Karen and Doug?   _____

3. Prof. Seidler, do you have a question?   _____

4. The strawberries and peaches look good today.   _____

5. Ann and Bob have left already.   _____

What is Meant by Tense?

The **tense** of a verb indicates the time when the action expressed by the verb takes place: at the present time, in the past, or in the future, for example.

I *am eating.*	PRESENT
I *ate.*	PAST
I *will eat.*	FUTURE

As you can see in the above examples, just by putting the verb in a different tense and without giving any additional information (such as "I am eating *now*," "I ate *yesterday*," "I will eat *tomorrow*"), you can indicate when the action of the verb takes, took, or will take place. There are six main tenses in English: present, present perfect, past, past perfect, future, and future perfect. This handbook discusses each of these tenses in separate sections.

What is the Present Tense?

The **present tense** indicates that the action is happening at the present time. It can be:

when the speaker is speaking	I *see* you.
a habitual action	He *smokes* when he *is* nervous.
a general truth	The sun *shines* every day.

In English: There are three forms of the verb which, although they have slightly different meanings, all indicate the present tense.

Mary *studies* in the library.	PRESENT
Mary *is studying* in the library.	PRESENT PROGRESSIVE
Mary *does study* in the library.	PRESENT EMPHATIC

In conversation, you automatically choose one of these three present-tense forms depending on what you want to say.

Where does Mary study?
She *studies* in the library.

Where is Mary studying now?
She *is studying* in the library.

Does Mary really study in the library?
Yes, she really *does study* in the library.

In German: There is only one verb form to indicate the present tense. This single form corresponds to the English present, present progressive, and present emphatic tenses. In German the present tense is indicated by the ending of the verb, without any helping or auxiliary verb such as *is* or *does* (see **What are Auxiliary Verbs?**, p. 92). It is very important, therefore, not to translate these English helping verbs. Simply put the main verb in the present.

Mary studies at the university.
studiert

Mary *is studying* at the university.
studiert

Mary *does study* at the university.
studiert

Practice

The following English sentences show different present forms of the verb *to play* in italics.
- Circle the words that correspond to the German present tense.
- Consult p. 84 to find the present-tense endings used to conjugate verbs in German.
- Using that chart, fill in the forms of the verb **spielen** (*to play*) that agree with the pronoun subjects given.

1. So John and Vera really do play tennis.   (pl.) sie_____

2. Yes, John plays often.   er_____

3. In fact, Vera is playing right now too.   sie_____

4. Our friends are playing with them.   (pl.) sie _____

5. Do you play too?   du_____

What is the Past Tense?

The **past tense** is used to express an action that occurred in the past.

In English: There are several verb forms that indicate that an action took place in the past.

I worked.	SIMPLE PAST
I was working.	PAST PROGRESSIVE
I did work.	PAST EMPHATIC

The simple past is called a **simple tense** because it consists of only one word. The past progressive and the past emphatic are called **compound tenses** because they consist of more than one word.

English also has three other compound tenses for expressing past actions. These are the perfect tenses.

I have worked.	PRESENT PERFECT
I had worked.	PAST PERFECT

These last two tenses will be discussed together with the future perfect in a separate section (see **What are the Perfect Tenses?**, p. 109).

In German: The two German tenses for expressing action in the past are the simple past and the perfect.

1. The **simple past** consists of only one word. This tense is also called the **imperfect (Imperfekt)** or the **preterite (Präteritum)**.

2. The German **perfect** tense (**Perfekt**) is a compound tense, consisting of two parts.

The formation of both the simple past and the perfect depends on whether the verb is a so-called strong verb or a weak verb. (See **What are the Principal Parts of a Verb?**, p. 73.) Your German textbook will explain in detail the formation of these two tenses for both groups of verbs.

It is important to remember that these two tenses have equivalent meanings. Their difference is one of style: generally, the perfect is used for a conversational style, and the simple past is used for narration.

Practice

I. Here are two English verbs in their infinitive form.
  • Fill in the three past tense verb forms we can use in English to indicate that an action has already taken place.

1. to write   I _____

           I _____

           I _____

2. to laugh   she _____

          she _____

          she _____

II. Below are pairs of sentences in German in the simple past and perfect tenses.
  • Write the simple past form in English. It is the translation that would usually be the best equivalent for these German verb tenses.

1. Sie sprachen.   They _____.
  Sie haben gesprochen.

           sprechen = to speak

2. Es regnete.   It _____.
   Es hat geregnet.

      regnen = to rain

3. Er telephonierte.   He _____.
   Er hat telephoniert.

         telephonieren = to telephone

What are Auxiliary Verbs?

A verb is called an **auxiliary verb** or **helping verb** when it helps another
verb to form one of its tenses (see **What is Meant by Tense?**, p. 87).
When it is used alone, it functions as a main verb.

Kit *is* a girl.	*is*	main verb
Tom *has* a headache.	*has*	main verb
They *go* to the movies.	*go*	main verb
They ***have gone*** to the movies. complete verb	***have*** ***gone***	auxiliary verb past participle of main verb
She ***has been gone*** for three hours. complete verb	***has*** ***been*** *gone*	auxiliary verb auxiliary verb past participle of main verb

In English: There are many auxiliary verbs, for example, *to have, to be,* and *to do.* They have three main uses:

1. to indicate the tense in the sentence (present, past, future—see **What is Meant by Tense?**, p. 87)

> Liz *is reading* a book.   PRESENT
> Liz *will read* a book.   FUTURE
> Liz *was reading* a book.   PAST

2. to help formulate questions

> Bob *has* a dog.   *has*   main verb
> *Does* Bob *have* a dog?   *does*   auxiliary verb
>   *have*   main verb

3. to indicate the passive voice (see **What is Meant by Active and Passive Voice?**, p. 204)

> The book *is read* by many people.

In German: The three main auxiliary verbs are **haben** (*to have*), **sein** (*to be*), and **werden** (*to become*).

1. **Haben** and **sein** are used as auxiliaries to form the perfect tenses of verbs. Some verbs use **haben** and some use **sein**. (See **What are the Perfect Tenses?**, p. 109.)

> Die Frau **hat** ihre Zeitung **gefunden.**
>   auxiliary verb   past participle of **finden**
>   **hat gefunden** (present perfect)

*The woman **has found** her newspaper.*
*The woman **found** her newspaper.*

Der Student ist sehr spät gekommen.

auxiliary verb   past participle of kommen

ist gekommen (present perfect)

*The student **has come** very late.*
*The student **came** very late.*

2. **Werden** is used to form the future tenses and the passive voice. (See **What is the Future Tense?**, p. 114, and **What is Meant by Active and Passive Voice?**, p. 204.)

Sie werden zahlen.

auxiliary verb   infinitive

werden zahlen (future tense)

*They **will pay**.*

Das Haus wird jetzt gebaut.

auxiliary verb   past participle of **bauen**

wird gebaut (passive voice, present tense)

*The house **is** now **being built**.*

USE OF AUXILIARIES IN ENGLISH AND IN GERMAN

You will find that German and English often do not overlap in their use of auxiliaries.

1. Equivalents for the English auxiliary verbs *do, does,* and *did* do not exist in German. When you encounter them in an English sentence which you are trying to express in German, you should use them as a guide to tense, but you must not translate them.

Do they *live here?*
　|　　　　|
ignore　　present-tense verb

Wohnen sie hier?
　|　　|　　|
live　they　here

2. English often uses present-tense forms of the verb *to be* (*is, are, am*) as an auxiliary verb with a present participle. (See **What is a Participle?**, p. 98.) German does not use this construction. Here again you should ignore the verb *are* and concentrate on the German equivalent of *work* in the present tense. (See **What is the Present Tense?**, p. 88.)

We are working today.
　　|　　　　|
auxiliary　　present
　verb　　participle

Wir **arbeiten** heute.
　|　　　|　　　|
we　work　today

MODAL AUXILIARIES

In English: There is a group of auxiliary verbs called **modal auxiliaries**. The word *modal* is related to *mode*, which means the manner of doing something. These modal verbs (e.g., *can, may, should, must*) show the attitude of the speaker toward what he or she is saying while the main verb indicates an action. In all the sentences below, the action expressed by the main verb (*read*) is not actually occurring; it is being discussed:

Chris *can read* this book.

> Chris has the ability to read the book.

Chris *may read* this book.

> Chris is allowed to read the book.

Chris *must read* this book.

Chris has to read the book.

Chris *should read* this book.

Chris ought to read the book.

In German: German also has a group of auxiliary verbs called modal auxiliaries: **können** (*to be able, can*), **sollen** (*to be supposed to, should*), **müssen** (*to be obligated to, must*), **dürfen** (*to be permitted to, may*), **wollen** (*to want to*), and **mögen** (*to like to*).[1] These are usually used with the infinitive of another verb.

Inge **will mitkommen.**

modal auxiliary   infinitive
present tense

Inge wants to come along.

Der Zug **sollte** pünktlich **ankommen.**

modal auxiliary   infinitive
past tense

The train was supposed to arrive on time.

When you learn the modal verbs in German, especially **wollen** and **mögen,** you will need to pay careful attention to their definitions because they are not always equivalent in meaning to English modal verbs. Your textbook will explain the meanings of the German modal verbs and give you examples of how they are used.

---

[1] The verb **lassen** (*to let, to allow*) is sometimes also grouped with the modal auxiliaries.

Practice

I. Circle the auxiliary verbs in the following English sentences.

1. They are working on the problem.

2. We can go now.

3. You do have a point.

4. She has been waiting a long time.

5. He will arrive later.

II. Some of the following English sentences contain verbal constructions that must be expressed differently in German.
- Circle the auxiliary verb + main verb in sentences where this construction appears to indicate verbal constructions that are different from those in German.
- Underline the verb in sentences that contain only a main verb to indicate that these sentences have an equivalent structure to German sentences.

1. The circus is coming to town.

2. Paul always reads the newspaper.

3. Maria drives too fast.

4. We are packing our bags.

5. Does Meg have everything?

What is a Participle?

A **participle** has two functions: 1. It is a form of the verb that is used in combination with an auxiliary verb to create certain tenses. 2. It may be used as an adjective or modifier to describe something.

> I *was writing* a letter.
> auxiliary   participle

> The *broken* vase was on the floor.
> participle describing vase

There are two types of participles: the **present participle** and the **past participle**. As you will see, participles are not used in the same way in English and German.

A. THE PRESENT PARTICIPLE

In English: The present participle is easy to recognize because it ends in **-ing**: work*ing*, study*ing*, danc*ing*, play*ing*, etc.

The present participle has various functions:

• in verb tenses

The present participle of the main verb is used with an auxiliary verb to form compound tenses.

> She is *singing*.
> present progressive

> They were *dancing*.
> past progressive

- attributive adjectives (see p. 170)

  This is an *amazing* discovery.

  describes the noun *discovery*

  Elise read an *interesting* book.

  describes the noun *book*

- participial phrases (see p. 217)

  Turning the corner, Tony ran into a tree.

  The phrase *turning the corner* describes Tony.

  Look at the cat *climbing the tree.*

  The phrase *climbing the tree* describes *cat.*

In German: The present participle is formed by adding **-d** to the infinitive.

INFINITIVE	PRESENT PARTICIPLE
singen	singend
spielen	spielend
sprechen	sprechend
schweigen	schweigend

USES OF THE PRESENT PARTICIPLE

In German the present participle occurs less frequently than in English and it is not used in the same way. Never assume that an English word ending with *-ing* is translated by its German counterpart ending in **-d.**

- in verb tenses

  As a beginner, you must keep in mind that the equivalents of English tenses formed with an auxiliary + present participle (*she is singing, they were dancing*) do not use participles in German. English constructions using participles simply correspond to particular German tenses of the verb, and these are often expressed with a single word.

> *She is singing.*
> Sie **singt.**
> |
>   present

> *They were dancing.*
> Sie **tanzten.**
> |
>   simple past

> *He will be writing.*
> Er **wird schreiben.**
> |_____|
>   future

- attributive adjectives

Like English, German often uses the present participle as an attributive adjective.

die **singenden** Kinder	*the singing children*
ein **spielendes** Mädchen	*a playing girl*
die laut **sprechende** Frau	*the loudly talking woman*

In such usage, the participle functions as any other attributive adjective and takes adjective endings. Look at **What is an Adjective?**, p. 169, for additional help and examples.

- in extended adjectival constructions

To modify nouns, formal German can use present participles in a group of words called an **extended adjectival construction**. This construction is similar to the participial phrase in English insofar as both structures use participles together with other words to give us information about a noun. An extended adjectival construction is generally placed before the noun it modifies and after the article, if there is one. In this construction, the present participle functions as an attributive adjective and takes the adjective endings.

Let us see how English and German can express thoughts using a present participle:

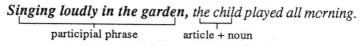

Singing loudly in the garden, the child played all morning.

   participial phrase   article + noun

In this English sentence, the participial phrase modifies the noun *child*.

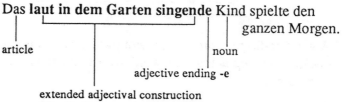

Das **laut in dem Garten singende** Kind spielte den ganzen Morgen.

article   noun

adjective ending -e

extended adjectival construction
"loudly in the garden singing"

In this German sentence, the extended adjectival construction modifies **Kind** (*child*).

PRESENT PARTICIPLE VERSUS GERUND

An English verb ending in -*ing* is not always a present participle; it can be a **verbal noun**. A verbal noun is a form of a verb which functions as a noun in a sentence. It is also often called a **gerund**. Since German verbal nouns differ in form from present participles, we will discuss them here so that you can learn to recognize them.

In English: A verbal noun ends in -*ing* and can function in a sentence in almost any way that a noun can. It can be a subject, direct object, indirect object, and an object of a preposition.

A word ending in *-ing* is a verbal noun, and not a present participle, if you can form a question by replacing that word with the interrogative *what*. The verbal noun will answer this one-word question.

> *Reading* can be fun.
> |
> noun from the verb *to read*
> subject of the sentence
>
> > Question: *What* can be fun?
> > Answer: Reading.

> We have often thought about *moving* away.
> |
> noun from the verb *to move*
> object of preposition *about*
>
> Question: *What* have we often thought about?
> Answer: Moving.

A word ending in *-ing* is a present participle when you must form a question by replacing that word with more than one word or the verb *to do*.

> We are *singing*.
> |
> present participle
>
> Question: *What* are we doing?
> Answer: Singing.

In German: Verbal nouns are usually expressed by a neuter noun made from the infinitive of the verb.

lesen	*to read*	das Lesen	*reading*
singen	*to sing*	das Singen	*singing*

You can recognize verbal nouns by identifying their function in a sentence. Since all German nouns are capitalized, you should be able to spot verbal nouns easily.

Wir **reden** viel.
|
verb

We are talking a lot.

Reden ist Silber, **Schweigen** ist Gold.
| | | |
verbal noun verb   verbal noun   verb

***Talking** is silver, **being silent** is gold.*
(Proverb: "Silence is golden.")

B. THE PAST PARTICIPLE

In English: This is the verb form you would use following *I have:* I have *talked,* I have *reached,* I have *taught.*

1. The "regular" verbs form their past participle by adding *-ed, -d,* or *-t* to the infinitive or dictionary form of the verb.

INFINITIVE	PAST PARTICIPLE
help	help*ed*
walk	walk*ed*
burn	burn*ed* or burn*t*

2. The "irregular" verbs form their past participle by changing their stem vowel (see p. 74) or by making other changes. Many of the most common English verbs are irregular.

INFINITIVE	PAST PARTICIPLE
go	gone
ride	ridden
speak	spoken

Notice that often, though not always, the past participle of irregular English verbs ends in *-n.*

The past participle is used:

- as a verb form in combination with the auxiliary verbs *have* or *be* to form verb tenses and to express the passive voice

  I *have written* all that I have to say.
  He *hasn't spoken* to me since our quarrel.
  Truer words *were* never *spoken*.
  This book *was written* several years ago.

- as an attributive adjective (see p. 170)

  Is the *written* word more important than the *spoken* word?

  Written describes the noun *word*.
  Spoken describes the noun *word*.

- as an adjective in a participial phrase (see p. 217)

  We didn't notice the sign *posted on the door.*

  The phrase *posted on the door* works as an adjective describing the noun *sign*.

In German: Past participles are formed differently depending on whether a verb is weak or strong (see **What are the Principal Parts of a Verb?**, p. 73). For both groups, however, the ge- prefix most commonly characterizes the past participle.

The weak verbs form their past participle according to a regular rule.

The strong verbs have irregular past participles.

1. The past participles of weak verbs are formed by adding

   - **ge-** to the front of the stem (unless the verb already begins with a prefix). Because it is placed before the stem it is called a **prefix,** see **What are Prefixes and Suffixes?**, p. 198.

- **-t** to the end of the stem. Because it is placed after the stem it is called a **suffix**.

INFINITIVE	STEM	PAST PARTICIPLE	
machen	mach-	gemacht	*made*
glauben	glaub-	geglaubt	*believed*

Some verb stems require slight adjustments. There are special rules for forming the past participle of verbs that already begin with prefixes and for verbs that end with the suffix *-ieren*. Your German textbook will explain how to handle these verbs.

2. The past participles of strong verbs often change the vowel in the stem, and occasionally some of the consonants. However, they all:

- add the **ge-** prefix to the front of the stem (unless the verb already begins with an inseparable prefix)

- end in **-en** (or, rarely, in **-n**)

INFINITIVE	PAST PARTICIPLE	
schlafen	geschlafen	*slept*
gehen	gegangen	*gone*
finden	gefunden	*found*
liegen	gelegen	*lain*

As you can tell from this list, there is no way to predict the past participle of a strong verb in German. You simply have to memorize it when the verb is presented in the vocabulary of your German textbook. It is important to remember, however, that the past participle of strong verbs always ends in **-en** (or **-n**), while the past participle of weak verbs always ends in **-t**. As with weak verbs, there are special rules for forming the past participle of strong verbs that already begin with a prefix.

Like English, German uses the past participle to form verb tenses, to express the passive voice, and as an attributive adjective:

- as a verb

  The most important use of the past participle in German is in verb combinations: all the perfect tenses are formed with an auxiliary verb, either **haben** (*to have*) or **sein** (*to be*) + the past participle. Look at **What are the Perfect Tenses?**, p. 109, for information on this use of the past participle.

  The passive voice is formed with the auxiliary verb **werden** (*to become*) + the past participle. Look at **What is Meant by Active and Passive Voice?**, p. 204, to learn more about this usage.

- as an attributive adjective

  In this usage, the rules about endings are the same as for any other attributive adjective. Look at **What is an Adjective?**, p. 169, for help in choosing the proper adjective ending.

  > **Ich verstehe die gesprochene Sprache** nicht.
  > *I do not understand the spoken language.*

  > **Die eingeladenen Gäste** sind alle gekommen.
  > *The invited guests all came.*

- as extended adjectival constructions

  To modify nouns, formal German can use past participles in a group of words as part of an extended adjectival construction. The extended adjectival construction is similar to the participial phrase in English insofar as both structures use participles together with other words to give us information about the nouns they describe. An extended adjectival construction with a past participle is generally placed before the noun it modifies and after the article, if there is one. When this occurs, the past participle functions as an attributive adjective and takes the adjective endings.

She sat down on the bench screwed to the wall.

participial phrase

In this English sentence, the participial phrase modifies the noun *bench.*

Sie setzte sich auf die **an die Mauer geschraubte** Bank.

article

adjective ending **-e**

noun

extended adjectival construction
"to the wall screwed"

In German, the extended adjectival construction modifies **Bank** (*bench*).

Practice

I. The following English sentences contain participles.
  • Circle the participles.
  • Indicate in the space provided whether each is a present or past participle.

	PRESENT	PAST
1. They are working late.		
2. Don't cry over spilled milk.		
3. Falling prices hurt farmers last month.		
4. There was a robin singing outside the window.		

	PRESENT	PAST

5. The treasure from the
   sunken ship was priceless.   _____ _____

6. It was a heated debate.   _____ _____

7. A turtle was basking in the sun. _____ _____

II. The following English sentences contain present participles and gerunds.
   - Underline the participles.
   - Circle the gerunds.

1. Flying will take less time than driving.

2. We are coming tomorrow.

3. Littering is prohibited.

4. This is a good place for sunbathing.

5. The leaves are turning red.

What are the Perfect Tenses?

The **perfect tenses** are compound tenses of the verb made up of an auxiliary verb + the past participle. (See **What is a Participle?**, p. 98.) We use the perfect tenses to express actions that took place in the past or to indicate the sequence of events.

I *have* not *seen* him.
auxiliary   past participle
  verb   of *to see*

They *had* already *gone*.
auxiliary   past participle
  verb   of *to go*

As you can see, the auxiliary verb *to have* can be put in different tenses: for example, *I have* is the present tense; *they had* is the past tense.

In English: There are three perfect tenses formed with the auxiliary verb *to have* + the past participle of the main verb. (See **What is a Participle?**, p. 98.)

The name of each perfect tense is based on the tense of the auxiliary verb.

1. **present perfect:** *to have* in the present tense + the past participle of the main verb.

I *have eaten.*
auxiliary   past participle
  verb   of *to eat*

They *have washed* the car.
auxiliary   past participle
  verb   of *to wash*

2. **past perfect** (pluperfect): *to have* in the simple past tense + the past participle of the main verb.

> I *had eaten* before 6:00.
> | |
> auxiliary   past participle
> verb   of *to eat*

> They *had washed* the car before the storm.
> | |
> auxiliary   past participle
> verb   of *to wash*

3. **future perfect:** *to have* in the future tense + the past participle of the main verb.

> I *shall have eaten* by 6:00.
> |_____| |
> auxiliary   past participle
> verbs   of *to eat*

> They *will have washed* the car by Thursday.
> |_____| |
> auxiliary   past participle
> verbs   of *to wash*

In German: As in English there are three perfect tenses; they are the perfect (**Perfekt**), the past perfect or pluperfect (**Plusquamperfekt**), and the future perfect, which occurs infrequently. They are all formed by the auxiliary verb **haben** (*to have*) or **sein** (*to be*) + the past participle. You must memorize which verbs require **sein** and which require **haben** as the auxiliary in the perfect tenses.

1. **Perfect tense: haben** or **sein** in the present tense + past participle of the main verb.

> Wir **sind** ins Kino **gegangen.**
> *We went to the movies.*

> Wir **haben** den Film **gesehen.**
> *We saw the film.*

Although this tense is structurally similar to the English present perfect, it is not used in the same way as the English present perfect. Often it is best translated into English by a simple past.

Ich **habe gegessen.**
I   *have*   *eaten*

I ate.
simple past

Sometimes an adverb of time will help you decide how to translate a German verb in the perfect tense.

Gestern habe ich zuviel gegessen.
***Yesterday** I ate too much.*
adverb of time simple past

(Awkward: "Yesterday I have eaten too much.")

Ich habe **schon** zuviel gegessen.
*I have **already** eaten too much.*
adverb of time present perfect

(Awkward: "I already ate too much.")

You will need to study your German textbook for more detailed explanations of the uses of the German perfect.

2. **Past perfect** or **pluperfect: haben** or **sein** in the simple past tense + past participle of the main verb. This tense resembles the English past perfect both in structure and in use. It expresses an action or condition that has ended before some other past action or condition.

Wir **waren** schon ins Kino **gegangen.**
simple past of **sein**

*We **had** already **gone** to the movies.*

Wir **hatten** den Film schon **gesehen.**

simple past of **haben**

*We **had** already **seen** the film.*

Notice how we can express the sequence of events by using different tenses:

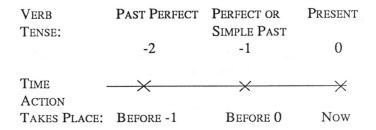

VERB TENSE:	PAST PERFECT	PERFECT OR SIMPLE PAST	PRESENT
	-2	-1	0

TIME ACTION TAKES PLACE:	BEFORE -1	BEFORE 0	NOW

*They **had** already **left** when I arrived.*
Sie **waren** schon **abgefahren,** als ich **ankam.**

pluperfect -2   simple past -1

*After we **had eaten**, we **took** a walk.*
Nachdem wir **gegessen hatten, machten** wir einen
Spaziergang.

pluferfect -2   simple past -1

3. **future perfect:** haben or sein in the future tense + past participle of the main verb.

Wir **werden** den Film **gesehen haben.**

future tense **haben**

*We **will have seen** the film.*

This tense is used like the English future perfect: It expresses an action which will be completed in the future before some other specific action or event occurs in the future.

VERB TENSE:	PRESENT 0	FUTURE PERFECT 1	FUTURE 2
TIME ACTION TAKES PLACE:	Now	AFTER 0 AND BEFORE 2	AFTER 0 AND 1

They will have left before I arrive.
Sie **werden abgefahren sein,** bevor ich ankomme.

        future perfect (1)   event in future (2)

Both action (1) and event (2) will occur at some future time, but action (1) will be completed before event (2) takes place. Therefore, action (1) is in the future perfect tense.

In the next section we will discuss the future tense. You will have to learn to recognize these tenses because they indicate the sequence in which events take place.

Practice

The following English sentences contain verbs in various tenses.
- Underline the complete verb in each part of the sentence.
- Beneath each sentence number the verbs to indicate the sequence in time when the action takes place:
    - 0 = present
    - -1 = simple past or present perfect
    - -2 = past perfect

1. After they had said goodbye, they climbed into the car.

_____

2. She wants to know who called last night.

_____

3. Before we saw the film we had read the book.

---

4. He asked what we had seen in Regensburg.

---

5. After we had finished cleaning up, we went home.

What is the Future Tense?

The **future tense** is used to describe an action which will take place in the future.

In English: The future tense is formed with the auxiliary verb *will* or *shall* + the main verb. Note that *shall* is used in formal English (and British English); *will* occurs in everyday language.

> Mary and Paul *will do* their homework tomorrow.
> I *shall go* out tonight.

In conversation, *shall* and *will* are often shortened to *'ll*: *they'll* do it tomorrow, *I'll* go out tonight.

Often the present tense is used in English to express a future action. When this occurs, an adverb helps express the sense of future time.

> We fly to Frankfurt *next week*.
> The semester ends *soon*.

In German: The future tense is formed by the auxiliary verb **werden** (literally *to become*) + the infinitive of the main verb. The conjugated verb **werden** agrees with the subject and the infinitive remains unchanged.

> Mary und Paul **werden** ihre Hausaufgabe **schreiben.**
> $\quad\quad\quad\quad$ 3rd per. pl. $\quad\quad\quad\quad\quad\quad\quad\quad$ infinitive
>
> *Mary and Paul will write their homework.*

> Ich **werde** heute abend **ausgehen.**
> $\quad$ 1st per. sing. $\quad\quad\quad\quad$ infinitive
>
> *I shall go out tonight.*

Note the word order in the above German sentences: the infinitive stands at the end of the sentence.

The future tense is used in two ways in German:

1. To express an action that will take place in the future.

> Wir **werden vorbeikommen.**
> $\quad\quad$ werden + infinitive **vorbeikommen**
>
> *We will come by.*

> Ich **werde anrufen.**
> $\quad\quad$ werden + infinitive **anrufen**
>
> *I will call.*

Quite often, however, German will use the present tense with an adverb of future time instead of using the future tense of the verb. We do this in English too, but less frequently.

Mary und Paul **schreiben morgen** ihre Prüfung.

   present tense adverb of future time

Mary and Paul are writing their test tomorrow.

Ich **gehe gleich** aus.

  present adverb of future time

I am going out soon.

2. To express an action that might take place in the future. In such usage, the future tense has no future meaning—it refers simply to a probability in the present time. This is sometimes called the **future of probability.**

The future of probability is usually expressed with the future tense and the adverbs **wohl** (*probably*), **sicher** (*certainly*), **wahrscheinlich** (*probably*), and **vielleicht** (*perhaps*) to express probability. In such sentences the German future tense is best translated with the English present.

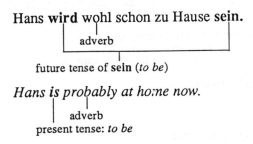

Hans **wird wohl** schon zu Hause **sein.**

   adverb

future tense of **sein** (*to be*)

Hans is probably at home now.

   adverb

present tense: *to be*

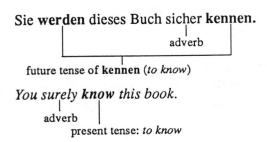

Sie **werden** dieses Buch sicher **kennen.**

     adverb

future tense of **kennen** (*to know*)

You surely know this book.

 adverb

present tense: *to know*

Practice

To help you think about the different ways in which German expresses the future and uses the future construction, look at these sentences in English.

- Underline the verbs in future tense.
- Circle the verbs in the present tense which are used with an adverb of future time.
- Box in the sentences which will use the future of probability in German.

1. Next week we are going on vacation.

2. Erica is probably downtown.

3. I shall return.

4. Only time will tell.

5. He'll be here in a minute.

6. The tickets probably cost a lot.

7. Are you leaving on Friday?

8. Temperatures will climb over the weekend.

9. Mark gets his driver's license tomorrow.

10. We'll certainly come right back.

What is Meant by Mood?

The word **mood** is a variation of the word *mode*, meaning manner or way. The mood is expressed by a form of the verb that indicates the attitude of the speaker toward what he or she is saying. As a beginning student of German, you need to know the names of the moods so that you will understand what your German textbook is referring to when it uses these terms. Verb forms are divided into moods, which, in turn, are then subdivided into one or more tenses. You will learn when to use the various moods as you learn verbs and their tenses.

In English: Verbs can be in one of three moods:

1. The **indicative mood** is used to indicate an action of the verb that really happens or is likely to happen. This is the most common mood, and most of the verb forms that you use in everyday conversation belong to the indicative mood.

    Robert *studies* German.
    Mary *is* here.

    The indicative mood occurs in the present tense (see p. 88), the past tense (see p. 90), and the future tense (see p. 114).

2. The **imperative mood** is used to express a command. The imperative mood does not have different tenses. (See p. 119.)

    Robert, *study* German now!
    Mary, *be* here on time!

3. The **subjunctive mood** is used to express an attitude or feeling about the action of the verb. Since it stresses feelings about what occurs in a sentence, it is "subjective." The subjunctive mood has different tense forms. (See **What is the Subjunctive?**, p. 122.)

    I wish she *were* here.
    If only we *knew* where they are.
    The teacher recommended that they *do* the exercise.

In German: These same three moods exist and have their own special forms. Although the indicative is the most common mood, as it is in English, the subjunctive is also very important. (See **What is the Subjunctive?**, p. 122.)

Practice

The following English sentences have *italicized verbs* in various moods.
- Imagine *how* a speaker might say each sentence.
- In the space provided, write the name for the verb's mood: indicative, imperative, or subjunctive.

1. Columbus *discovered* America. _____

2. We wish you *were* here. _____

3. *Come* into the house, children! _____

4. We *have* bats in the attic. _____

5. They *had forgotten* their hats. _____

6. He suggested that she *call* again. _____

7. *Look* at that! _____

What is the Imperative?

The **imperative** is the mood of the verb used for commands. It is used to give someone an order.

In English: There are two types of commands:

1. The you-**command** is used when giving an order to one person or many persons. The dictionary form of the verb is used for the *you*-command.

> *Answer* the phone.
> *Clean* your room.
> *Talk* softly.

Notice that the pronoun "you" is not stated in these sentences, although it could be included for special emphasis (i.e., You clean your room right now!). The absence of the pronoun *you* in a sentence is a good indication that you are dealing with an imperative and not the present indicative mood.

2. The we-**command** is used when the speaker gives an order to himself as well as to others. In English this command begins with the phrase "let's" followed by the dictionary form of the verb.

> *Let's leave.*
> *Let's go* to the movies.

In German: The same two types of imperatives exist.

1. The *you*-command has three different forms, according to the three different personal pronouns for you: **du, ihr,** and **Sie** (see **What is a Personal Pronoun?**, p. 50). In all forms except the **du**-form, the verb is the same as the present-tense indicative. In written German an exclamation point is used after an imperative.

In the two familiar forms of the imperative, the subject pronoun is usually dropped, as in English:

> **du**-form
> **Höre!**[1]   *Listen.*
> **Schreibe** mir bald!   *Write me soon.*

---

[1] The final **-e** on **höre** and **schreibe** is optional in conversational German, though mandatory when the verb stem ends in **-t, -d,** or **-ig.**

ihr-form

Kommt mit!	*Come along.*
Eßt nicht so schnell, Kinder!	*Don't eat so fast, children.*

In the formal form, the subject pronoun is included; it is placed directly after the **Sie**-form of the present tense.

Sie-form

Sprechen Sie lauter!	*Speak more loudly.*
Kommen Sie mit!	*Come along.*

2. In the *we*-command, the subject pronoun is included; it is placed directly after the **wir**-form of the present tense.

wir-form

Gehen wir jetzt!	*Let's go now.*
Sprechen wir Deutsch!	*Let's speak German.*

Your German textbook will explain in detail the rules for forming the imperative.

Practice

Here are some imperatives in English.
- On the line provided, indicate the imperative form you would use when translating these sentences into German: **du, ihr, Sie,** or **wir.**

FORM

1. Hurry up, Chris. _____

2. Let's go to the movies. _____

3. Close the door, children. _____

4. Excuse me a minute, Dr. Benn. _____

5. Please pick up your room, Ann. _____

What is the Subjunctive?

The **subjunctive** is the mood of the verb which is used to express actions and states that are not actual fact. We often say that these actions are "unreal" or "contrary to fact," that is, that they are imaginary or hypothetical. Notice the difference between the indicative mood (used to express facts) and the subjunctive mood in the following examples:

INDICATIVE

- States a fact

    Kathy *is* here.

- States a real possibility, something that can be a fact

    If Kathy *is* here, you can meet her.

    Implication: There is a real possibility that Kathy is here, and therefore that you can meet her.

SUBJUNCTIVE

- Expresses something that is unreal, **contrary to fact**

    If Kathy *were* here, you could meet her.

    Implication: Kathy is not here, and you cannot meet her. Therefore this sentence is contrary to fact.

- Expresses a wish, i.e., a hypothetical condition

    I wish Kathy *were* here.

    Implication: But she is not. Therefore this sentence expresses a hypothetical condition.

• Expresses necessity or demand

> We asked Kathy to *be* here so that we can meet her.
>
> Implication: She is not here now and we are not certain that she
> will be here, but we urged her to come so that we could meet her.

In English: The subjunctive is difficult to recognize because it
resembles tenses in the indicative. For this reason we do not always
recognize it as the subjunctive when we use it.

The subjunctive mood can be expressed in two different ways in the
present, depending on the type of sentence in which it is used.

1. One present subjunctive form is derived from the simple past
   form of the indicative. The contrast between the simple past
   indicative and the present subjunctive is most evident in the verb
   to be in the 1st and 3rd persons singular.

TO BE

SIMPLE PAST		PRESENT SUBJUNCTIVE	
I	was	I	were
you	were	you	were
he, she, it	was	he, she it	were
we	were	we	were
you	were	you	were
they	were	they	were

With other verbs, you will have to rely on the meaning of the
sentence to determine whether the verb is in the indicative or
subjunctive mood because the simple past indicative and present
subjunctive forms are identical.

To Speak

SIMPLE PAST		PRESENT SUBJUNCTIVE	
I	spoke	I	spoke
you	spoke	you	spoke
he, she, it	spoke	he, she, it	spoke
we	spoke	we	spoke
you	spoke	you	spoke
they	spoke	they	spoke

The present subjunctive occurs most commonly in two types of sentences:

- Conditions contrary to fact

    These sentences are made up of two clauses, the if-clause and the conclusion:

    if clause   conclusion

    If I *were* in Europe now, I would visit Vienna.

    The verb of the if-clause is in the subjunctive; the verb of the conclusion clause, i.e. *would* + the dictionary form of the main verb, is in what is often called the **conditional.**

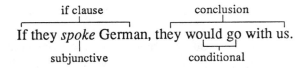

if clause   conclusion

If they *spoke* German, they would go with us.

subjunctive   conditional

- Expressions of wishes

    I wish I *were* in Europe right now.

    subjunctive

If only we *spoke* German fluently!
        |
      subjunctive

Notice that the verb *wish* is used only in the first example. In the second example the wish is implied and the verb is in the subjunctive mood.

2. Another subjunctive form is identical to the dictionary entry. This form is used with verbs for asking, urging, demanding, or requesting. Let us see how this form compares with the present indicative.

She *comes* to see me every week.
     |
   fact
   present indicative of the verb *to come*

I asked that she *come* see me every week.
 | |
demand   present subjunctive
              (infinitive: *to come*)

He *is* here.
  |
 fact
 present indicative of the verb *to be*

It is necessary that he *be* here.
               |
   demand   present subjunctive
              (infinitive: *to be*)

In German: The German subjunctive has both a present and a past tense. German subjunctive forms are much easier to identify than English ones because they are usually different from the German indicative forms. As in English, there are two different types of subjunctives, one derived from the simple past of the verb and one derived from the infinitive, but their usage is not the same as the usage of the two English subjunctive forms. In this section we will discuss only the first type, the so-called **general subjunctive** or **subjunctive II**, which has a present and a past tense. The other, less common, type of subjunctive is discussed in the section **What is Meant by Direct and Indirect Discourse?**, p. 132.

A. General Subjunctive (Subjunctive II)— Forms

Like English, German derives the general subjunctive form from the simple past form of the indicative.

Present Subjunctive

Basically the present-tense general subjunctive is formed by using the indicative past stem of the verb + subjunctive endings. The past stem of the verb is the stem to which you add the personal endings when you conjugate a verb in the simple past tense.

INFINITIVE		PAST TENSE INDICATIVE 3rd PER. SING.		PAST STEM
sagen	*to say*	sagte	*said*	sagt-
schlafen	*to sleep*	schlief	*slept*	schlief-

Let us look at one simple example that shows the endings used to form the subjunctive in German:

INFINITIVE		PAST TENSE		PAST STEM
gehen	*to go*	ging	*went*	ging-

PRESENT GENERAL SUBJUNCTIVE

ich	ginge
du	gingest
er/sie/es	ginge
wir	gingen
ihr	ginget
sie/Sie	gingen

THE *WÜRDE*-CONSTRUCTION

German also has a two-word construction, called the **würde**-construction, which often replaces the one-word general subjunctive forms in spoken German. The **würde**-construction is formed by the present general subjunctive form of **werden** (literally *to become*) + the infinitive.

ich	würde	gehen
du	würdest	gehen
er/sie/es	würde	gehen
wir	würden	gehen
ihr	würdet	gehen
sie/Sie	würden	gehen

PAST SUBJUNCTIVE

The past subjunctive is a compound tense and resembles the German past perfect, except that the auxiliary verb (**haben** or **sein**) is in the subjunctive rather than in the indicative.[1]

ich	hätte	gesagt
du	hättest	gesagt
er/sie/es	hätte	gesagt
wir	hätten	gesagt
ihr	hättet	gesagt
sie/Sie	hätten	gesagt
ich	wäre	gekommen
du	wärest	gekommen
er/sie/es	wäre	gekommen
wir	wären	gekommen
ihr	wäret	gekommen
sie/Sie	wären	gekommen

[1] Note that while the indicative mood in German has three tenses to express actions in the past (past, perfect, and past perfect), the subjunctive mood has only one past form.

As a student of German, you will need to learn many details about general subjunctive usage and the verb forms that are exceptions. Your textbook will give you a detailed explanation of all the subjunctive forms and the special rules you need to follow in using them.

B. GENERAL SUBJUNCTIVE—USAGE

The general subjunctive in German is commonly used in three kinds of sentences:

- Expressions contrary to fact

   Unlike English, where the subjunctive is used only in the *if*-clause, in German the subjunctive is also used in the conclusion where the English verb is in the *would*-construction, i.e., the conditional.

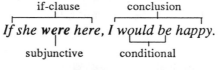

   Wenn sie hier **wäre,** dann **wäre** ich glücklich.
   subjunctive subjunctive

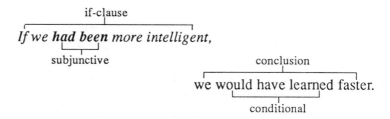

Wenn wir intelligenter **gewesen wären,**
_{subjunctive}

dann **hätten** wir schneller **gelernt.**
_{subjunctive}

- Expressions of wishes

    Unlike English, where the subjunctive is used only in the con-
    clusion of the wish-statement, in German the verb *wish* is also in
    the subjunctive.

    I wish she were here!
    indicative subjunctive

    Ich **wünschte,** sie **wäre** doch hier!
    subjunctive   subjunctive

    I wish I were in Europe now!
    indicative subjunctive

    Ich **wünschte,** ich **wäre** jetzt in Europa!
    subjunctive   subjunctive

- polite requests

    Could you do me a favor?
    Könntest du mir einen Gefallen **tun?**
    subjunctive   infinitive

    Would you please open the door.
    Würden Sie bitte die Tür **aufmachen.**
    subjunctive   infinitive

THE *WÜRDE*-CONSTRUCTION

In structure, German sentences using the **würde**-construction resemble sentences in English formed using *would* + the dictionary form of the main verb, i. e., the conditional (see p. 124).

Ich **würde gehen,** wenn ich Zeit hätte.

subjunctive of **werden**   subjunctive of **haben**
+ infinitive **gehen**

I would go if I had time.

Sie **würden** dich **einladen,** wenn sie könnten.

subjunctive of **werden**   subjunctive of **können**
+ infinitive **einladen**

They would invite you if they could.

Note that in both English and German this subjunctive structure resembles the future indicative construction. See **What is the Future Tense?**, p. 114.

FUTURE INDICATIVE	SUBJUNCTIVE
I will go.	*I would go.*
Ich **werde gehen.**	Ich **würde gehen.**
present of **werden**	subjunctive of **werden**

Your textbook will explain when you should use this construction and when you must use the one-word general subjunctive forms.

As you learn more German, you will discover various other situations in which the subjunctive is used. Although its use does not always resemble that of the English subjunctive, being aware of the subjunctive in English can often help you use it correctly in German.

Practice

I. Here are several English sentences in the indicative and subjunctive moods.
- Look at the *italicized* verbs.
- In the space provided indicate whether the statement is a statement of fact (F) or contrary to fact (CTF).

1. West Germany *is* approximately the size of Oregon. _____

2. I wish I *were finished* already. _____

3. If I *had* wings, I *would fly* away. _____

4. Since things *are going* smoothly,
   we *will be done* soon. _____

5. If they had come earlier, we *could
   have gone* for a walk. _____

II. These English sentences are in the subjunctive mood and contain subjunctive verb forms.
- Underline the verbs.
- In the space provided, identify the tense you would use to express these sentences in German by writing *present* or *past*.

1. If only Reinhard were back! _____

2. Students would do their homework if they had time. _____

3. If we had planned ahead, we would have
   packed warmer clothes. _____

4. I would like a glass of mineral water. _____

5. If it were colder, I would wear gloves. _____

6. If she had called, I would have come.   _____

7. If only the rain had stopped already!   _____

III. The following sentences contain verbs in the indicative and subjunctive moods.
   • Box in the verbs in indicative mood.
   • Underline the subjunctive verbs.

1. They wish they were rich.

2. Would you please comment on that question.

3. If you only knew what you are missing!

4. We would like to go, but we don't have time.

5. I would have been here sooner if the traffic had not been tied up.

What is Meant by Direct and Indirect Discourse?

Direct discourse is the transmission of another person's statement or message by direct quotation. Direct discourse is usually set in quotation marks.

> Mary said, "I am going to Berlin."
> John asked, "What will you do in Berlin?"

The words that appear in quotation marks are what you would hear if you eavesdropped on the conversation.

Indirect discourse is the transmission of another person's statement or message without quoting her or his words directly. Indirect discourse reproduces the substance of the message but does not use quotation marks. Furthermore, it changes the speaker's first-person pronoun ("*I am going...*") to agree logically with the perspective of the person speaking ("*She* was going...").

> Mary said she was going to Berlin.
> John asked what she would do in Berlin.

If you were reporting a conversation you overheard, you would automatically change the pronouns in this manner. This is what happens in indirect discourse.

In English: Indirect discourse is often indicated by a shift in tense.

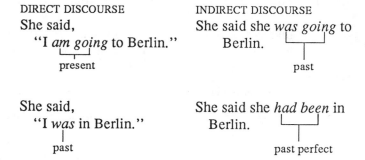

DIRECT DISCOURSE	INDIRECT DISCOURSE
She said,	She said she *was going* to
"I *am going* to Berlin."	Berlin.
present	past
She said,	She said she *had been* in
"I *was* in Berlin."	Berlin.
past	past perfect

In German: Indirect discourse is indicated by a shift in mood from the indicative to the subjunctive. There is a **special subjunctive** called the **indirect discourse subjunctive** or **subjunctive *I*** it is used primarily for indirect discourse in writing. In conversation the general subjunctive or subjunctive II is often used for indirect discourse.

Let us look at how German uses both the special subjunctive and the general subjunctive to express indirect discourse in the present and past tenses.

The present tense of the special subjunctive is formed by the infinitive stem + the subjunctive endings. It can be replaced by the present general subjunctive form of the verb.

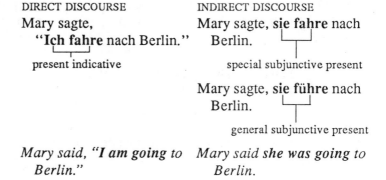

The past tense is formed by the special subjunctive form of the helping verb (**haben** or **sein**) + the past participle of the main verb.

Your German textbook will explain in greater detail the formation and use of the special indirect discourse subjunctive.

Practice

I. The following sentences contain quotations that are direct discourse.
- Underline the verb that is in direct discourse.
- On the line to the right of the sentence, indicate whether the verb describes an action in the present or in the past time.
- Box in any pronouns or possessive adjectives within the quotation that change when you rewrite these sentences in indirect discourse.

- In the spaces provided, rewrite these direct discourse sentences as indirect discourse.

PRESENT OR PAST

1. She asked, "How is the weather?"

   She asked _____   _____

2. They shouted, "We found the trail."

   They shouted that _____   _____

3. He announced, "I just got my driver's license."

   He announced that _____   _____

4. Libby said, "I'm coming."

   Libby said that _____   _____

5. Tony called out, "I'm done."

   Tony called out that _____   _____

II. Below are five sentences in indirect discourse.
   - Underline the verb that occurs in the main part of the sentence, following the introduction "she said...," etc.
   - Circle the pronouns and possessive adjectives in that part of the sentence.
   - Now rewrite these sentences as statements in direct discourse, changing the pronouns and verb forms as necessary.

1. Jane said she was studying.

   Jane said, "_____."

2. A spokesman said that the Senate had ratified the treaty.

    A spokesman said, "_____."

3. Peter commented that he was tired.

    Peter commented, "_____."

4. Hansel and Gretel said they had been lost.

    Hansel and Gretel said, "_____."

5. The child whispered that she had hidden her toy.

    The child whispered, "_____."

What is a Possessive Pronoun?

A **possessive pronoun** is a word that both replaces a noun and indicates the possessor of that noun. The word *possessive* comes from *possess*, to own.

> Whose house is that? It's *mine*.

Mine is a pronoun that replaces the words *my house* and shows who possesses that noun.

In English: Here is a list of the English possessive pronouns:

SINGULAR
1st PERSON	mine	
2nd PERSON	yours	
3rd PERSON	his	*(masculine)*
	hers	*(feminine)*
	its	

PLURAL

1st PERSON	ours
2nd PERSON	yours
3rd PERSON	theirs

Possessive pronouns refer primarily to the possessor; they never change their form, regardless of the thing possessed.

Is that your house? Yes, it is *mine*.
Are those your keys? Yes, they are *mine*.

The same possessive pronoun (*mine*) is used, although the objects possessed are different in number (*house* is singular; *keys* is plural).

John's car is blue. *His* is blue.
Mary's car is blue. *Hers* is blue.

Although the object possessed is the same (*car*), the possessive pronoun is different because the possessor is different (*John* is masculine singular; *Mary* is feminine singular).

In German: As in English, the possessive pronouns refer to the possessor, but they also must agree in case, gender, and number with the noun they replace. The stems used to form the possessive pronouns are as follows:

SINGULAR

1st PERSON	mein-	
2nd PERSON	dein-	
3rd PERSON	sein-	(*masculine*)
	ihr-	(*feminine*)
	sein-	(*neuter*)

PLURAL

1st PERSON	unser-	
2nd PERSON	euer-	
	Ihr-	(*formal*)
3rd PERSON	ihr-	

As a beginning student, you should learn to recognize possessive pronouns when they occur in sentences. The forms of the possessive pronouns are essentially the same as those of the possessive adjectives (see **What is a Possessive Adjective?**, p. 181), but the endings are slightly different. Furthermore, a possessive pronoun stands by itself in a sentence while the possessive adjective precedes a noun.

POSSESSIVE ADJECTIVE   POSSESSIVE PRONOUN
Das ist **mein** Buch.   Das ist **meins.**
    adjective noun   pronoun

*That is **my** book.*   *That is **mine.***

Hier ist **unser** Bleistift.   Hier ist **unserer.**
    adjective   noun   pronoun

*Here is **our** pencil.*   *Here is **ours.***

Practice

Circle the possessive pronouns in the following sentences.

1. I have my book; do you have yours?

2. Did your parents come? Ours stayed home.

3. Whose meal was the best? Hers was.

4. Did somebody forget this jacket? Yes, it's his.

5. Let me see those keys: I bet they're mine.

What is a Reflexive Pronoun?

A **reflexive pronoun** is a pronoun which refers back to the subject of the sentence: it *reflects* the meaning back to the subject. Both the subject and the pronoun refer to the same person(s), thing(s), or idea(s).

In English: Reflexive pronouns end with *-self* in the singular and *-selves* in the plural:

	SUBJECT PRONOUN	REFLEXIVE PRONOUN
SINGULAR	I	myself
	you	yourself
	he	himself
	she	herself
	it	itself
PLURAL	we	ourselves
	you	yourselves
	they	themselves

Reflexive pronouns agree in person and number with their antecedents (and in gender with *he, she,* and *it*). This is because the reflexive pronoun and the subject refer to the same person, thing, or idea.

> I washed *myself.*
> Mark and Gretchen helped *themselves* to dessert.

Although the subject pronoun *you* is the same for the singular and plural, there is a difference in the reflexive pronouns used to refer to these subjects: *yourself* is used when speaking to one person (singular) and *yourselves* is used when speaking to more than one person (plural).

> Molly, did you make *yourself* a sandwich?
> Children, make sure *you* dry *yourselves* properly.

A reflexive pronoun can have various functions in a sentence. It can be:

- the direct object

> I cut *myself* with the knife.
> | |
> subject   direct object

>> Who cut herself with the knife? I did.
>> *I* is the subject of the sentence.

>> Whom did I cut with the knife? Myself.
>> *Myself* is the direct object of the verb *cut*.

> I can't help *myself*.
> | |
> subject   direct object

>> Who can't help himself? I can't.
>> *I* is the subject of the sentence.

>> Whom can I not help? Myself.
>> *Myself* is the direct object of the verb *help*.

- the indirect object

> You should write *yourself* a note.
> | |
> subject   indirect object

>> Who should write herself a note? You should.
>> *You* is the subject of the sentence.

>> To whom should you write a note? To yourself.
>> *Yourself* is the indirect object of the verb *write*.

>> What should you write yourself? A note.
>> *Note* is the direct object of the verb *write*.

- the object of a preposition

> He thinks only of *himself*.
> | |
> subject   object of preposition

> Who thinks only of himself? He does.
> *He* is the subject of the sentence.

> Of whom does he think? Of himself.
> *Himself* is the object of the preposition of.

> You talk about *yourself* too much.
> | |
> subject   object of preposition

> Who spoke about her? You did.
> *You* is the subject of the sentence.

> About whom did you speak? About yourself.
> *Yourself* is the object of the preposition *about*.

In German: As in English there are reflexive pronouns for each of the different personal pronouns (1st, 2nd, and 3rd persons, singular and plural). The German reflexive pronouns, however, have both an accusative form (for direct objects and for prepositions that require the accusative) and a dative form (for indirect objects and for prepositions that require the dative). Depending on the verb or the preposition, you will choose either the accusative reflexive pronoun or the dative reflexive pronoun.

NOMINATIVE SUBJECT PRONOUN	ACCUSATIVE REFLEXIVE PRONOUN	DATIVE REFLEXIVE PRONOUN	
ich	mich	mir	*myself*
du	dich	dir	*yourself*
er/sie/es	sich	sich	*himself* *herself* *itself*
wir	uns	uns	*ourselves*
ihr	euch	euch	*yourselves*
sie	sich	sich	*themselves*
Sie	sich	sich	*yourself/-selves*

Like English reflexive pronouns, German reflexive pronouns are used as objects of verbs and as objects of prepositions. In both instances you will need to pay attention to the case required. Remember that the case of the reflexive pronoun depends on its function in the German sentence, not the English sentence. Pay special attention to verbs that take a direct object in English, but require a dative case in German.

- the direct and indirect objects of a German verb

    *I cut **myself** with the knife.*
    direct object of *cut*

    Ich habe **mich** mit dem Messer geschnitten.
    subject   accusative object of **habe geschnitten**

    *You should write **yourself** a note.*
    indirect object of *write*

    You should write *to whom*? To yourself.

    Du solltest **dir** einen Zettel schreiben.
    subject   dative   accusative object
                   object

    *I can't help **myself**.*
    direct object of *help*

    Remember: to help = **helfen** + dative

    Ich kann **mir** nicht helfen.
    subject   dative object of **helfen**

- the object of a preposition

    *He thinks only of **himself**.*
                                    |
                        object of preposition *of*

    Remember: to think of = **denken an** + accusative

    Er denkt nur an **sich**.
      | |
    subject   accusative object of **denken an**

    *You talk about **yourself** too much.*
                           |
                object of preposition *about*

    Remember: to talk about = **reden von** + dative

    Du redest zuviel von **dir**.
     | |
    subject   dative object of **von**

Practice

Fill in the proper reflexive pronoun.

1. Ruby, you should feel free to make _____ at home.

2. We fixed the car _____.

3. He picked everything up by_____.

4. She wanted some time to _____.

5. I wish I'd thought of that _____.

6. Steve and Maura, you should get _____ ready.

What is a Reflexive Verb?

A **reflexive verb** is a verb conjugated with a reflexive pronoun. (See **What is a Reflexive Pronoun?**, p. 139.)

In English: Many verbs can take on a reflexive meaning by adding a reflexive pronoun.

> Peter *cuts* the paper.
> |
> regular verb

> Peter *cuts himself* when he shaves.
> |_____|
> |
> verb + reflexive pronoun

There are very few verbs, however, that require a reflexive pronoun to complete their meaning. Verbs which can have a reflexive pronoun as their object can also have other nouns or pronouns as their object.

> I hurt *myself*.
> |
> reflexive pronoun as direct object

> I don't like to hurt *people*.
> |
> noun as direct object

> Please, calm *yourself*.
> |
> reflexive pronoun as direct object

> The soft music calmed his *nerves*.
> |
> noun as direct object

In German: There are some verbs that must have reflexive pronouns to complete their meaning. These verbs are called **reflexive verbs**. The English equivalents of these verbs do not have reflexive pronouns; for example:

sich erhohlen	*to recover*
sich befinden	*to be located*
sich verlieben	*to fall in love*

As you can see, the infinitive of these verbs is always given with the third person reflexive pronoun, **sich**. When you conjugate a reflexive verb, you will have to select the correct reflexive pronoun since it changes as the subject changes. Notice that the verb **sich erhohlen** (*to recover*), conjugated below in the present tense, takes the accusative form of the reflexive pronoun.

SUBJECT PRONOUN	VERB	REFLEXIVE PRONOUN
ich	erhole	mich
du	erholst	dich
er	erholt	sich
sie	erholt	sich
es	erholt	sich
wir	erholen	uns
ihr	erholt	euch
sie	erholen	sich
Sie	erholen	sich

Reflexive verbs can be conjugated in all tenses. The subject pronoun and reflexive pronoun remain the same regardless of the verb tense; only the verb form changes.

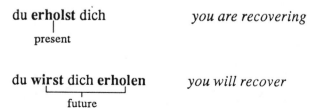

du **erholst** dich   *you are recovering*
 │
present

du **wirst** dich **erholen**   *you will recover*
 └─────────┬─────────┘
       future

du h<u>a</u>st dich erh<u>o</u>lt   *you recovered*

<u>   </u>
       perfect

As you learn new vocabulary, you will need to memorize which German verbs are reflexive, that is, which ones require the reflexive pronoun as part of the whole verb. A number of verbs can be used with or without reflexive pronouns, and sometimes verbs have a different meaning when they are reflexive. Your German textbook will introduce you to these verbs.

Practice

Here is a conjugation of the German reflexive verb **sich freuen über** (*to be happy about something*).
- Using the sample conjugation on p. 145, fill in the accusative reflexive pronouns you must use.

ich freue   _____

du freust   _____

er/sie/es freut   _____

wir freuen   _____

ihr freut   _____

sie/Sie freuen   _____

What is an Interrogative Pronoun?

An **interrogative pronoun** is a word that replaces a noun and introduces a question. Interrogative comes from *interrogate*, meaning to question.

In English: Different interrogative pronouns are used depending on whether you refer to a "person" (this category includes human beings and live animals) or a "thing" (this category includes objects and ideas). In addition, the interrogative pronoun referring to persons changes according to its function in the sentence.

A. PERSONS

Who is the nominative form and stands for the subject of the sentence:

> *Who* lives here?
> |
> subject

> *Who* wrote that book?
> | |
> subject   direct object

> *Who* will help you?
> | |
> subject   direct object

Whom is the objective form and is used as the object of a verb or, in standard written English, as the object of a preposition (See **What are Objects?**, p. 33).

> *Whom* do you know here?
> | |
> direct object subject

> From *whom* did you get the book?
> | | |
> preposition object   subject
>   of preposition

In spoken or colloquial English we often use the nominative case *who* instead of the objective case *whom*. In colloquial English the two sentences above would be as follows:

>Who do you know here?
>Who did you get the book from?

Whose is the possessive form and is used in questions about possession or ownership:

>I found a pencil. *Whose* is it?
>I have Mary's paper. *Whose* do you have?

B. THINGS

What refers only to things, and the same form is used for subject, direct object, indirect object, and the object of a preposition.[1]

>*What* happened?
>subject

>*What* do you want?
>direct object

>*What* did you cook with?
>object of preposition *with*

In German: As in English, different interrogative pronouns are used when referring to persons and when referring to things. In addition, the form of an interrogative pronoun depends on its case, i.e., the function it has in a sentence. (Number and gender do not affect the interrogative pronoun.) Let us look at the interrogative pronouns referring to persons first because they are more complicated.

---

[1] Do not confuse with "*What* book is on the table?" where *what* is an interrogative adjective. See p. 185.

A. PERSONS

You will have to determine the proper case form. To do this, you must recognize the pronoun's function in the sentence.

1. Is it the subject of the question?
2. Is it the object of the verb? Does that verb take the accusative or the dative?
3. Is it the indirect object of the verb?
4. Is it the object of the preposition? Does that preposition take the accusative or the dative?
5. Is it the possessive pronoun *whose*?

Here are examples of the interrogative pronoun in each of the 5 functions listed above.

1. *who* (subject) = **wer** (nominative)

> *Who is in the room?*
> *The teacher is in the room.*
>
>> Function of *who*: subject of *is*
>> Case in German: nominative
>
> **Wer** ist in dem Zimmer?
> Die Lehrerin ist in dem Zimmer.

> *Who is coming this evening?*
> *Hans and Inge are coming.*
>
>> Function of *who*: subject of *is coming*
>> Case in German: nominative
>
> **Wer** kommt heute abend?
> Hans und Inge kommen.

As you can see, **wer** can refer to both singular and plural subjects. Number and gender do not affect the interrogative pronouns in German.

2. *who(m)* (object) = **wen** (accusative)
                        wem (dative)

The interrogative pronoun used as an object is harder for you to identify in English because the *whom* form (the correct form) has been replaced by *who* in everyday language. Therefore, you will have to analyze the English sentence carefully to find the grammatical function of *who(m)*. You will also need to determine whether the German sentence requires the accusative or dative case.

> *Who did you see?* ⟶ *Whom did you see?*
>
> Function of *who*: direct object of *see*
>   *You* is the subject of *see*.
>
> Case: German verb **sehen** (*to see*) requires an accusative object.

Wen sehen Sie?
|
accusative

> *Who is Peter visiting?* ⟶ *Whom is Peter visiting?*
>
> Function of *who*: direct object of *is visiting*
>
> Case: German verb **besuchen** (*to visit*) requires an accusative object.

Wen besucht Peter?
|
accusative

> *Who are they helping?* ⟶ *Whom are they helping?*
>
> Function of *who:* direct object of *are helping*
> *They* is the subject of are *helping*.
>
> Case: German verb **helfen** (*to help*) requires a dative object.

Wem helfen sie?
|
dative

Who can I believe? ⟶ *Whom can I believe?*

Function of *who*: direct object of *can believe*

Case: German verb **glauben** (*to believe*) requires a
dative personal object.

Wem kann ich glauben?
|
dative

3. *who(m)* (indirect object) = **wem** (dative)

Who is she sending a letter to?[1] ⟶
To whom is she sending a letter?

Function of *who*: indirect object of *is sending*
She is the subject of *is sending*.
A letter is the direct object.
Case: dative

Wem schickt sie einen Brief?

Who did you tell the story to? ⟶
To whom did you tell the story?

Function of *who*: indirect object of *did tell*
You is the subject of *did tell*.
The story is the direct object.
Case: dative

Wem hast du die Geschichte erzählt?

The word **wem** itself means "to whom" or "for whom" an action
is done, thus when it functions as an indirect object we do not
need a preposition to complete its meaning as we do in English
when we express the same idea.

---

[1] If you restructure the dangling preposition, it will help you identify the indirect object in
these sentences (see p. 158). The indirect object explains "to whom," "to what," or "for what"
the action of the verb takes place.

4. *who(m)* (object of a preposition) =
preposition + **wen** (accusative)
preposition + **wem** (dative)

When asking a question about the object of a preposition in German, you must include the preposition in the question. To help you do this, restructure the dangling preposition in the English sentence so that it precedes the interrogative pronoun (see p. 192).

> *Who is he talking about?* ──────▸ *About whom is he talking?*
>
>> Function of *who*: object of preposition
>> *He* is the subject of *is talking*.
>> Case: **Von** (*about*) requires a dative object.

Von wem spricht er?

> *Who are we going with?* ──────▸ *With whom are we going?*
>
>> Function of *who*: object of preposition
>> *We* is the subject of *are going*.
>> Case: **Mit** (*with*) requires a dative object.

Mit wem gehen wir?

> *Who are you doing that for?* ──▸ *For whom are you doing that*
>
>> Function of *who*: object of preposition
>> *You* is the subject of *are doing*.
>> Case: **Für** (*for*) requires an accusative object.

Für wen machst du das?

> *Who is she waiting for?* ──────▸ *For whom is she waiting?*
>
>> Function of *who*: object of preposition
>> *She* is the subject of *is waiting*.
>> Case: **Warten auf** (*to wait for*) requires an accusative object.

Auf wen wartet sie?

5. *whose* (possessive) = **wessen** (genitive)

This form should present no problems since the English form *whose* can be identified easily and there is only one form in German.

> ***Whose** pencil is that?*
> **Wessen** Bleistift ist das?

> ***Whose** house did you buy?*
> **Wessen** Haus habt ihr gekauft?

B. THINGS

There is only one interrogative pronoun for asking about things; the German equivalent of *what* is **was**. The same form is used for the nominative, dative, and accusative cases, and no distinction is made between the singular and the plural.

> ***What** is in this package?*
> |
> subject

> **Was** ist in diesem Paket?
> |
> nominative

> ***What** are you doing?*
> |
> direct object

> **Was** machst du?
> |
> accusative

Practice

The following English sentences contain interrogative pronouns.
- Underline the interrogative pronouns.
- Provide the information requested about their use.
- Write the appropriate German interrogative pronoun using the clues given.

1. Who read the book?

   Function: _____

   Type of antecedent (person or thing): _____

   _____ hat das Buch gelesen.

2. What did she say?

   Function: _____

   Type of antecedent: _____

   _____ hat sie gesagt?

3. Whose car is that?

   Function: _____

   Type of antecedent: _____

   _____ Auto ist das?

4. Who(m) does he know?

   Function: _____

   Type of antecedent: _____

   _____kennt er?

5. Who are we waiting for?

Restructured: _____

Function: _____

German verb: **warten auf** + accusative

Type of antecedent: _____

Auf _____warten wir?

What is a Relative Pronoun?

A **relative pronoun** is a word that serves two purposes:

1. As a pronoun it stands for a noun or another pronoun that has been mentioned previously. The noun or pronoun it refers to is called its **antecedent**.

> This is the boy *who* broke the window.
> |
> antecedent

2. It introduces a **relative clause.** A relative clause is a type of dependent (or subordinate) clause, that is, a group of words having a subject and a verb separate from the subject and verb of the main sentence. (See **What is a Clause?**, p. 218.) A dependent clause cannot stand alone as a complete sentence.

main clause   dependent clause

This is the boy *who* broke the window.

subject   verb

"Who broke the window" is not a complete sentence.

In this sentence *who* is a relative pronoun introducing the relative clause. The relative clause gives us additional information about the antecedent *boy*.

In English and in German, the selection of the relative pronoun will depend on the function of the relative pronoun in the relative clause. You must train yourself to go through the following steps:

1. Find the relative clause.

2. Determine the function of the relative pronoun in the relative clause.
   • Is it the subject?
   • Is it the direct object?
   • Is it the indirect object?
   • Is it the object of a preposition?
   • Is it a possessive modifier?

3. Select the proper relative pronoun based on steps 1 and 2.

In English: The selection of most relative pronouns depends on the function of the relative pronoun in the relative clause, and on whether the antecedent is a person or not. Here are the most common English relative pronouns:

A. SUBJECT OF THE RELATIVE CLAUSE

Refers to a person: *who*

This is the student *who* answered all the time.

antecedent

Who is the subject of *answered*.

Refers to a thing: *which*

> The plan, *which* was approved, is controversial.
> |
> antecedent
>
> *Which* is the subject of *is*.

Refers to a person or a thing: *that*

> This is the book *that* is so popular.
> |
> antecedent
>
> *That* is the subject of *is*.

B. OBJECT OF THE RELATIVE CLAUSE

These pronouns are often omitted in English. We have indicated them in parentheses because they cannot be omitted in German.

Refers to a person: *whom*

> This is the student (*whom*) I saw yesterday.
> | |
> antecedent   subject of relative clause
>
> *Whom* is the direct object of *saw*.

Refers to a thing: *which*

> This is the book (*which*) I bought.
> | |
> antecedent   subject of relative clause
>
> *Which* is the direct object of *bought*.

Refers to a person or a thing: *that*

> This is the book (*that*) I read.
> | |
> antecedent   subject of relative clause
>
> *That* is the direct object of *read*.

C. Indirect Object or Object of a Preposition in the Relative Clause

Refers to a person: *whom*

> Here is the student I gave the present to.
>
> antecendent   subject of relative clause

> This English structure cannot be translated word-for-word into German for two reasons: 1. the German language does not permit dangling prepositions (see p. 192), and 2. the relative pronoun omitted in English must be expressed in German. To establish the German structure, you must restructure the English sentence, inserting the preposition within the sentence and adding a relative pronoun. If you are not sure where to place the preposition and the relative pronoun, remember that they follow immediately after the antecedent.

> Spoken English ⟶ Restructured
>
> Here is the student   Here is the student
> I gave the present *to*.   *to whom* I gave the present.
>
> *Whom* is the indirect object of *gave*.

> Here is the student I was talking *about*.
>
> antecedent

> As is the case with indirect objects, spoken English often omits the object of a preposition when it is a relative pronoun and places the preposition at the end of the sentence. Again, you will have to restructure the sentence.

Spoken English   ⟶   Restructured

Here is the student I was speaking *about*.	Here is the student *about whom* I was speaking.

Whom is the object of the preposition about.

Refers to a thing: *which*

Here is the museum they gave a painting *to*.
         |
      antecedent

Spoken English   ⟶   Restructured

Here is the museum they gave the painting *to*.	Here is the museum *to which* they gave the painting.

Which is the indirect object of *gave*.

D. POSSESSIVE MODIFIER *WHOSE*

The possessive modifier *whose* is a relative pronoun that does not change its form regardless of its function or antecedent.

Here are the people *whose* car was stolen.
        | |
   antecedent   possessive modifying *car*

Look at the house *whose* roof was fixed.
        | |
   antecedent   possessive modifying *roof*

USE OF RELATIVE PRONOUNS

Relative clauses are very common. We use them in our everyday speech without giving much thought to why and how we construct them. Relative pronouns allow us to combine in a single sentence two thoughts that have a common element.

Let us look at a few examples to see how we construct relative clauses:

- Sentence A: That is the player.
  Sentence B: He won the game.

1. Identify the element the two sentences have in common.

   > *The player* and *he;* both refer to the same persons.
   > *The player* (sentence A) is the antecedent. *He* (sentence B) will be replaced by a relative pronoun.

2. Establish the function of the relative pronoun in the relative clause. It will have the same function as the word it replaces.

   > The relative pronoun will be the subject of *won*. (*He* is the subject of *won*.)

3. Choose the appropriate relative pronoun according to whether its antecedent is a person or a thing.

   > *Who* is the relative pronoun referring to persons.

4. Place the relative pronoun after its antecedent.

   > That is the player *who* won the game.
   >   antecedent   relative clause

- Sentence A: The German teacher is new.
  Sentence B: I met her today.

  1. Common element: *the German teacher* and *her*
  2. Function of *her*: direct object
  3. Antecedent: *The German teacher* is a person. We can use *whom* as a relative pronoun.
  4. Placement: *whom* after *the German teacher*

  The German teacher, *whom* I met today, is new.
          antecedent   relative clause

In spoken English, you would say: "The German teacher I met today is new." Notice that the relative pronoun *whom* is left out, making it difficult to identify the two clauses.

- Sentence A: They had read the book.
  Sentence B: I was speaking about it.

    1. Common element: *book* and *it*
    2. Function of *it:* object of the preposition *about*
    3. Antecedent: *The book* is not a person. We use the relative pronoun *which.*
    4. Placement: *about which* after *the book*

They had read the book *about which* I was speaking.

        antecedent   relative clause

In spoken English, you would say: "They had read the book I was speaking about." Notice that the preposition comes at the end of the sentence and that there is no relative pronoun.

In German: Like nouns, the German relative pronouns have four different case forms (nominative, accusative, dative, and genitive). The case used depends on the function of the pronoun in the relative clause. In German, it does not matter whether the antecedent is a person or a thing: the same set of relative pronouns refers to both. What is important is the gender and number of the antecedent; this will determine the gender and the number of the relative pronoun. The various forms of the relative pronoun are very similar to the forms of the definite article (**der, die, das**). Look at your German textbook to learn these forms.

Remember that although the relative pronouns *who, whom, that,* and *which* are often omitted in English, they must always be stated in German. In English we can say either "Is that the house *that* Jack built?" or "Is that the house Jack built?" We can also say, "Is there anyone here *who(m)* you know?" or "Is there anyone here you know?" In German, since the relative pronoun can never be omitted, only the first sentence in each of these pairs is possible.

To find the correct relative pronoun in German you must go through the following steps:

1. Recognize the relative clause; restructure the English clause if there is a dangling preposition. (See p. 158.)

2. Find the antecedent: to what word in the main clause does the relative clause refer? (Don't forget that the antecedent is always the noun that precedes the relative pronoun.)

3. Determine the number and gender of the antecedent.
   - Is it singular or plural?
   - If it is singular, is it masculine, feminine, or neuter? (There is only one plural for the three genders.)

4. Determine the function and therefore the case of the relative pronoun within the relative clause:

		CASE
• Is it the subject?	=	nominative
• Is it a direct object?	=	accusative
• Is it a dative object?	=	dative
• Is it an indirect object?	=	dative
• Is it the object of a preposition?		

What case does the preposition take?	=	accusative dative genitive

• Is it a possessive modifier?		genitive

5. Select the proper form based on steps 1-4.

Let us apply the steps outlined above to the following sentences in order to select the correct relative pronoun:

*The man **who** visited us was nice.*

1. Relative clause: *who visited us*
2. Antecedent: *man*
3. Number and gender of antecedent: **Der Mann** (*the man*) is masculine singular.
4. Function of *who* within relative clause: subject = nominative
5. Selection: masculine singular nominative **der**

Der Mann, **der** uns besuchte, war nett.

*Is **that** the bike you bought?*

1. Relative clause: *(that) you bought*
   Remember that the relative pronoun must always be stated in German.
2. Antecedent: *the bike*
3. Number and gender of antecedent: **Das Rad** (*the bike*) is neuter singular.
4. Function of *that* within relative clause: direct object = accusative
5. Selection: neuter singular accusative **das**

Ist das das Rad, **das** du gekauft hast?

*Hans, **whose** alarm clock was broken, overslept.*

1. Relative clause: *whose alarm clock was broken*
2. Antecedent: Hans
3. Number and gender of antecedent: Since *Hans* is the name of one man or boy, it is masculine singular.
4. Function of *whose* within the relative clause: possessive modifier connecting *Hans* with his *alarm clock* = genitive
5. Selection: masculine singular genitive **dessen**

Hans, **dessen** Wecker kaputt war, hat sich verschlafen.

Here are those books you were talking about.

SPOKEN ENGLISH   ⟶   RESTRUCTURED

Here are those books you were talking *about*.	Here are those books *about which* you were talking.

1. Relative clause: *about which you were talking*
2. Antecedent: *books*
3. Number and gender of antecedent: **Die Bücher** (*the books*) is neuter plural. (With plurals the gender is not important, because there is only one set of plural forms for all three genders.)
4. Function of *which* within relative clause: object of preposition *about*. **Von** always takes a dative object.
5. Selection: neuter plural dative **denen**

Hier sind die Bücher, **von denen** Sie geredet haben.

Relative pronouns are difficult to handle, and this handbook provides only a simple outline. Refer to your German textbook for further help.

RELATIVE CLAUSES WITH INDEFINITE ANTECEDENTS

In all of the above examples, we can identify one particular noun or pronoun in the main clause as the antecedent of the relative clause. When no such single antecedent is clearly apparent, the relative clause is said to have an indefinite antecedent.

In English: We avoid using relative pronouns which do not have a definite antecedent, especially in standard written English.

Anna invited us all, which we found nice.
              main clause   relative clause

Here we have a relative clause, but there is no clear antecedent. The relative clause refers to the entire idea expressed in the main clause.

In German: It is perfectly acceptable to consider an entire clause as the antecedent of the relative clause. In such sentences the same relative pronoun is always used: **was.**

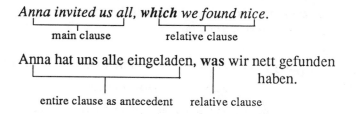

There are other instances in German which require the use of **was** as a relative pronoun. Your German textbook will show you when you must use **was.**

RESTRICTIVE CLAUSES VERSUS NON-RESTRICTIVE CLAUSES

In English: The punctuation of relative clauses reflects a distinction between those clauses which are "restrictive" and those which are "non-restrictive."

1. **Restrictive clause**—A clause that restricts or limits the meaning of the antecedent; such a clause is essential to the meaning of the sentence and cannot be omitted without changing the sense of the whole sentence. It is not set off from the rest of the sentence by commas. A restrictive clause is introduced by *who, whom, which,* or *that.*

   Do you know the girl *who* won the prize?
                       | |
                  antecedent relative clause

   The relative clause is essential to identify the antecedent, *the girl.* Thus the clause is restrictive and is not set off by commas.

2. **Non-restrictive clause**—A clause that is not essential to the meaning of the sentence and which could be omitted without losing the sentence's basic meaning. It is set off from the rest of the sentence by commas. A non-restrictive clause is introduced by *who, whom, whose,* or *which;* the relative pronoun *that* belongs in restrictive clauses.

My friend John, *whom* you met last week, is here.

antecedent   relative clause

The relative clause is not essential to identify the antecedent; it merely gives additional information about *my friend John.* Thus the clause is non-restrictive and must be set off by commas.

Often in your own writing you can decide only from the context of the sentence whether a relative clause is restrictive or non-restrictive.

In German: All German relative clauses are separated by commas from the main clause of the sentence. As far as punctuation is concerned, there is no distinction between restrictive and non-restrictive clauses.

Practice

I. Here are some English sentences containing relative clauses.
- Underline the relative pronoun.
- Circle its antecedent.
- Identify the function of the relative pronoun by circling the appropriate letter(s):

subject (S)
direct object (DO)
indirect object (IO)
object of a preposition (OP)
possessive modifier (PM)

1. I received the letter that you sent me.   S   DO   IO   OP   PM

2. Those are the people who speak German.   S   DO   IO   OP   PM

3. The woman whom you met left today.   S   DO   IO   OP   PM

4. This is the book whose title I forgot.   S   DO   IO   OP   PM

5. Kit is the student about whom I spoke.   S   DO   IO   OP   PM

II. The following pairs of English sentences contain common elements.
   • Fill in the information requested to find the relative pronoun you should use.
   • On the line below, write a new English sentence using a relative pronoun.

1. The dog is friendly. It lives next door.

   Common elements: _____

   Antecedent: _____

   Element replaced by relative pronoun: _____

   Function of element replaced: _____

   Relative pronoun: _____

_____

2. The Smiths left for Austria. You met them in Basel.

Common elements: _____

Antecedent: _____

Element replaced by relative pronoun: _____

Function of element replaced: _____

Relative pronoun: _____

_____

3. The new student is German. You were asking about her.

Common elements: _____

Antecedent: _____

Element replaced by relative pronoun: _____

Function of element replaced: _____

Relative pronoun: _____

_____

What is an Adjective?

An **adjective** is a word that describes a noun or a pronoun.

In English: Adjectives are classified according to the way they describe a noun or pronoun.

- A **descriptive adjective** indicates a quality. It answers the question *what kind?*

    > The house was *large*.
    > The woman is *intelligent*.
    > The *small* child plays in front of the *red* house.
    > They are *nice*.

- A **possessive adjective** shows to whom or to what something belongs. It answers the question *whose?* See p. 181.

    > *His* book is lost.
    > *Our* parents are away.

- An **interrogative adjective** forms a question about someone or something. It asks *which?* or *what?* See p. 185.

    > *What* book is lost?
    > *Which* newspaper do you want?

- A **demonstrative adjective** points out someone or something. It answers the question *which one?*

    > *This* teacher is excellent.
    > *That* question is very appropriate.

In all these cases, it is said that the adjective *modifies* the noun or pronoun.

In German: Adjectives are identified in the same way as in English. The form that an adjective takes, however, depends on the case, gender, and number of the noun it modifies. We will discuss descriptive, possessive, and interrogative adjectives in separate sections of this handbook. Your German textbook will introduce demonstrative adjectives, which you should learn as vocabulary items.

What is a Descriptive Adjective?

A **descriptive adjective** is a word that indicates a quality of a noun or pronoun. As the name implies, it *describes* the noun or pronoun.

There are two types of descriptive adjectives: attributive adjectives and predicate adjectives.

1. **Attributive adjectives** are adjectives which appear before the noun they modify.

> the sm<u>a</u>ll child
> attributive adjective
>
> the r<u>e</u>d house
> attributive adjective

2. **Predicate adjectives** are adjectives which accompany a linking verb (see **What is a Predicate Noun?**, p. 41), often a form of the verb *to be*. Predicate adjectives modify the subject of the sentence.

> The child is sm<u>a</u>ll.
> predicate adjective
>
> The house is r<u>e</u>d.
> predicate adjective

In English: Descriptive adjectives have only one form, whether they are used as attributive or predicate adjectives.

The small child sat in the sandbox.

attributive adjective modifying *child*

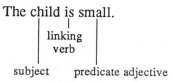

The child is small.

linking verb

subject   predicate adjective

The red house is for sale.

attributive adjective modifying *house*

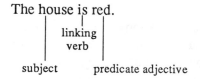

The house is red.

linking verb

subject   predicate adjective

The tired mother put her feet up.

attributive adjective modifying *mother*

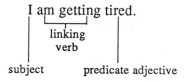

I am getting tired.

linking verb

subject   predicate adjective

In German: The form a descriptive adjective takes depends on whether it is used as an attributive adjective or as a predicate adjective. Attributive adjectives take special adjective endings; predicate adjectives do not.

To find the proper ending for an attributive adjective in German, you must ask yourself the following questions:

1. What is the gender of the noun—is it masculine, feminine, or neuter?
2. Is the noun singular or plural in number?
3. What is the case of the noun—nominative, accusative, dative, or genitive?
4. Is the noun preceded by a definite article, an indefinite article, or no article at all?

German adjectives take different sets of endings depending on how the case, gender, and number of a noun are indicated by the preceding article. Briefly, an adjective will have explicit, i.e., "strong" endings, when the article does not fully indicate the case, gender, and number, or when there is no article. An adjective will take "weak" endings, i.e., less explicit ones, when the article itself clearly indicates case, gender, and number.

Once you can answer these questions, you will be able to choose the appropriate ending for a given adjective. Your German textbook will show you the various types of endings you need to know, and you must practice and memorize them until you can use the correct one automatically.

Let us look at a few examples so that you can see how to analyze adjectives in sentences.

*The **small** child plays in front of the house.*

> Adjective = **klein** (*small*)
> Gender: **Das Kind** (*the child*) is neuter.
> Number: singular
> Case: nomininative
> Article: definite **das**

Das kleine Kind spielt vor dem Haus.
      |
    nominative
   singular neuter
preceded by definite article

*A child plays in front of **a red door**.*

> Adjective = **rot** (*red*)
> Gender: **Die Tür** (*the door*) is feminine.
> Number: singular
> Case: **vor** showing location takes dative
> Article: indefinite **eine** (dative form = **einer**)

Ein Kind spielt vor **einer roten** Tür.

dative
feminine singular
preceded by indefinite article

Old wine is expensive.

> Adjective = **alt** (*old*)
> Gender: **Der Wein** (*the wine*) is masculine.
> Number: singular
> Case: nominative
> Article: none

Alter Wein ist teuer.

nominative
masculine singular
not preceded by article

Predicate adjectives in German have the same form as the dictionary entry for the adjective regardless of the gender and number of the nouns or pronouns they modify.

The children are small.
Die Kinder sind **klein**.

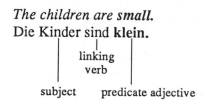

The house is red.
Das Haus ist **rot**.

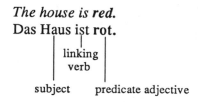

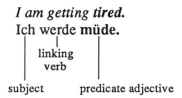

I am getting tired.
Ich werde **müde.**

subject   predicate adjective

linking
verb

Practice

I. The following English sentences contain adjectives.
- Underline each adjective.
- Draw an arrow from the adjective to the noun or pronoun described.

1. You can't teach an old dog new tricks.

2. We were tired after our long walk.

3. This meal is excellent.

4. Dark clouds rose above the high mountains.

5. Which sports are popular in Europe?

II. Here are sentences with different types of adjectives.
- Underline all predicate adjectives.
- Box in the attributive adjectives, remembering that in German these attributive adjectives take special endings.

1. The red onions and green peppers look fresh.

2. New cars have gotten very expensive.

3. The younger children seemed tired.

4. The old castle is impressive.

5. Good friends are hard to find.

What is Meant by Comparison of Adjectives?

When we speak about two or more nouns that have the same quality, we use **comparison** to indicate that one of these nouns or pronouns has a greater, lesser, or equal degree of this quality. The adjective that indicates what is being compared changes its form when we compare adjectives.

```
                comparison of adjectives
            ┌───────────────┴───────────────┐
        Meg is tall but Todd is taller.
              │                    │
        adjective modifying    adjective modifying
        the noun Meg           the noun Todd
```

There are two degree or forms of comparison: **comparative** and **superlative**.

In English: Let us go over what is meant by the different types of comparison and how each type is formed.

An adjective in its positive form refers to the quality of one person or thing.

> Mary is *pretty*.
> My house is *big*.
> His car is *expensive*.
> This book is *interesting*.

1. The comparative form compares the quality of one person or thing with the same quality in another person or thing. The comparison can indicate that one or the other has more, less, or the same amount of the quality.

   The comparison of greater degree (more) is formed by:

   • short adjective + *er* + *than*

   > Peter is tall*er than* Anita.
   > Beth is pretti*er than* her sister.

- *more* + long adjective + *than*

    This book is *more* interesting *than* that one.
    My car is *more* dependable *than* your car.

The comparison of lesser degree (less) is formed by:

- *not as* + adjective + *as,* or *less* + adjective + *than*

    Meg is *not as* tall *as* Todd.
    Our car is *less* dependable *than* your car.

The comparison of equal degree (same) is formed by:

- *as* + adjective + *as*

    Jane is *as* tall *as* Mark.
    My car is *as* expensive *as* your car.

2. The superlative form is used to stress the highest or lowest degree of quality.

The superlative of highest degree is formed by:

- *the* + short adjective + *-est*

    Mary is *the* pretti*est i*n the family.
    My car is *the* saf*est* on the market.

- *the most* + long adjective

    That argument was *the most* convincing.
    This book is *the most* interesting of all.

The superlative of lowest degree is formed by:

- *the least* + adjective

> Eric is *the least* tired.
> This radio is *the least* expensive of all.

A few adjectives do not follow this regular pattern of comparison. You must use an entirely different word for the comparative and the superlative.

ADJECTIVE:	This apple is good.
COMPARATIVE:	This apple is better.
	not "gooder"
SUPERLATIVE:	This apple is the best.
	not "goodest"

In German: There are the same two types of comparison of adjectives as in English.

1. The comparative of predicate and attributive adjectives is basically formed by adding **-er** to the stem of the adjective. The spelling of some adjectives also changes slightly in the comparative and superlative forms. Your textbook will explain these changes.

A predicate adjective just adds **-er**. This form corresponds to the comparative of many short English adjectives.

> Maris is **jünger** als ihr Bruder.
> jung + -er
>
> *Maria is younger than her brother.*

Das Buch is **interessanter** als der Film.
|
interessant + -er

*The book is **more interesting** than the film.*

An attributive adjective adds *-er* + the proper adjective ending. Your German textbook will explain in detail the various endings and how to select one.

ADJECTIVE STEM

jung   Ich kenne das jüngere Mädchen nicht.
|
comparative -er + adjective ending -e

*I don't know the **younger** girl.*

interessant   Das ist ein interessanterer Film.
|
comparative -er + adjective ending -er

*That is a **more interesting** film.*

German also has several irregular comparatives just as English does; for example:

ADJECTIVE		COMPARATIVE	
gut	*good*	besser	*better*
viel	*much*	mehr	*more*

You will find a list of irregular comparatives in your German textbook which you will have to memorize.

2. The superlative degree of the adjective is formed by adding -st to the adjective stem (-est if the adjective stem ends in -d, -t, -z, -s, or -ß).

There are small differences in the way the superlative adjective is used depending on whether it is a predicate adjective or an attributive adjective.

The predicate adjective takes the two-word form **am** + adjective + **-st** + **-en**.

Inge ist **am kleinsten.**
klein + -st + -en
Inge is the smallest.

Dieses Buch is **am neuesten.**
neu + -est + -en
This book is the newest.

Im Winter ist das Wetter **am kältesten.**
kalt + -est + -en
In winter the weather is (the) coldest.

The attributive adjective is preceded by the definitive article (**der, die, das**) and has the appropriate adjective ending that corresponds to the case, number, and gender of the noun it modifies. Thus the form it takes is article + adjective + **-st** + adjective ending.

Inge ist **das kleinste** Mädchen in der Schule.
definite article   klein + -st + -e
Inge is the smallest girl in the school.

Die Schallplatten sind alle neu,
aber diese ist **die neueste.**
definite article   neu + -est + -e

Schallplatte is the unstated but implied final word in the sentence, modified by **die neueste.**

The records are all new, but this is the newest one.

Some superlatives are irregular and will have to be memorized; the same adjectives that are irregular in the comparative are irregular in the superlative:

POSITIVE		SUPERLATIVE	
gut	*good*	am besten	*best*
viel	*much*	am meisten	*most*

Consult your German textbook for a full list of irregular forms.

Practice

I. Using the words given, write sentences with comparative adjectives. The various degrees of comparison are indicated as follows:
+ greater degree
− lesser degree
= equal degree
++ superlative

1. The teacher is / (+) old / the students.

_____

2. This student is / (=) intelligent / that one.

_____

3. Kathy is / (-) tall / Molly.

_____

4. This movie is / (++) good / this season.

_____

5. Today is / (++) hot / day on record.

_____

II. The following sentences contain phrases with adjectives printed in italics.
- If the phrase includes an attributive adjective, circle AA.
- If you could translate the phrase into German using a predicate adjective, circle PA.

1. The Rhine is *the busiest river* in Europe.   AA   PA

2. These exercises are *shorter.*   AA   PA

3. This song is *more popular.*   AA   PA

4. Let's build *a better mousetrap.*   AA   PA

5. Whales are *the largest mammals.*   AA   PA

What is a Possessive Adjective?

A **possessive adjective** is a word that describes a noun by showing who "possesses" the noun being discussed. The owner is called the "possessor" and the noun modified is called the person or thing "possessed."

In English: Here is a list of the possessive adjectives:

SINGULAR
    1st PERSON   my
    2nd PERSON   your
                      his
    3rd PERSON   her
                      its
PLURAL
    1st PERSON   our
    2nd PERSON   your
    3rd PERSON   their

The possessive adjective refers only to the possessor; it does not agree in gender or number with the noun it modifies.

Mary's bike is new.   *Her* bike is new.
    | |
possessor   noun possessed

    John's room is neat.   *His* room is neat.
    The cat's ears are short.   *Its* ears are short.

In German: Unlike English, where possessive adjectives refer only to the possessor, German possessive adjectives refer to both the possessor and to the possessed. The possessive adjective itself refers to the person who possesses. The ending on the possessive adjective, however, agrees in case, gender, and number with the noun possessed.

Here are the steps you should follow to choose the correct possessive adjective and its proper form:

1. Indicate the possessor.

	GERMAN EQUIVALENT (nominative)
my	mein
your (familiar singular)	dein
his	sein
her	ihr
its	sein
our	unser
your (familiar plural)	euer
their	ihr
your (formal)	Ihr

2. Identify and analyze the noun possessed:

What is its gender?
What is its number?
What is its case?

3. Provide the ending for the possessive adjective which corresponds to the case, gender, and number of the noun possessed. These endings are the same as those for the indefinite articles, **ein, eine,** and **ein.** Your textbook will show you the various endings.

Let us look at some examples:

> *He always forgets his books.*
>
> 1. Possessor: *his* = sein
> 2. Noun possessed: *books*
> Gender: **Das Buch** (*book*) is neuter.
> Number: *Books* is plural.
> Case: **Vergessen** (*to forget*) takes a direct object = accusative.
> 3. Ending: -e
>
> Er vergißt immer **seine** Bücher.
> |
>   accusative
>   neuter plural

> *She gives her brother the telephone number.*
>
> 1. Possessor: *her* = **ihr**
> 2. Noun possessed: *brother*
> Gender: **Der Bruder** (*brother*) is masculine.
> Number: **Bruder** is singular.
> Case: Indirect object of **geben** (*to give*) = dative
> (She gives her number *to whom?* Her brother.)
> 3. Ending: -em
>
> Sie gibt **ihrem** Bruder die Telefonnummer.
> |
>   dative
>   masculine singular

Once you have memorized the endings well, you will be able to perform this whole process automatically.

Practice

I. In the following sentences:
- Underline the possessive adjective.
- Circle the noun possessed.

1. The students took their exams home.

2. Susan put on her coat and her scarf.

3. Tom put his comb in his pocket.

4. Bob met her brother.

5. Molly knows his sister.

II. The following examples show you how to find the correct form of German possessive adjectives.
- Fill in the missing information requested.
- Underline the possessive adjective in the German sentence.
- Circle the case ending on the German possessive adjective.

1. I am looking for *my* key.

Possessor: _____

Noun possessed: _____

Gender: **Der Schlüssel** (*key*) is masculine.

Number: _____

Case: **Suchen** (*to look for*) takes a
direct object = _____

Ending: **-en**

Ich suche **meinen** Schlüssel.

2. We are helping *your* aunt.

Possessor: _____

Noun possessed:_____

   Gender: **Die Tante** (*aunt*) is_____

   Number:_____

   Case: **Helfen** (*to help*) requires a dative object.

   Ending: **-er**

Wir helfen **deiner** Tante.

What is an Interrogative Adjective?

An **interrogative adjective** is a word that asks a question about a noun.

In English: The words *which* and *what* are called interrogative adjectives when they come in front of a noun and are used to ask a question. The form of the interrogative adjective never changes regardless of the function of the noun it modifies.

> *Which* book is for sale?
> |
>   subject
>
> *What* courses are you taking?
> |
>   direct object
>
> About *what* film are you talking?
> |
> object of the preposition *about*

In German: There is only one interrogative adjective to ask "which" or "what" in German. Like all adjectives, the interrogative adjective must agree in case, gender, and number with the noun it modifies.

The singular nominative forms are:

MASCULINE	welcher
FEMININE	welche
NEUTER	welches

The endings are the same as for the definite article, **der, die, das,** except in the neuter singular nominative and accusative where the ending **-es** replaces **-as.**

Let us analyze a few examples to see how the interrogative adjective is used in German.

> *Which lamp is cheaper?*
>
>> Gender: **Die Lampe** (*lamp*) is feminine.
>> Number: singular
>> Case: Subject of **sein** (*to be*) = nominative
>
> **Welche** Lampe ist billiger?

> *Which (what) dress do you want to wear?*
>
>> Gender: **Das Kleid** (*dress*) is neuter.
>> Number: singular
>> Case: Direct object of **tragen** (*to wear*) = accusative
>
> **Welches** Kleid willst du tragen?

> *Which man do we give our tickets to?*
>
>> Gender: **Der Mann** (*man*) is masculine.
>> Number: singular
>> Case: Indirect object of **geben** (*to give*) = dative
>> (**Karten** is the direct object.)
>
> **Welchem** Mann geben wir unsere Karten?

If the noun modified is the object of a preposition, you must include the preposition in the construction of the question, because the preposition determines the case of the interrogative adjective. When you form a question regarding the object of a preposition, you must use a more formal structure consisting of the preposition + interrogative adjective + noun.

To obtain the formal English that is equivalent to the German sentence, restructure the question to eliminate the dangling preposition of the conversational English construction.

> **Which** *street does he live on?*
>
>> Restructured: *on which* street does he live
>> Gender: **Die Straße** (*street*) is feminine.
>> Number: singular
>> Case: Object of preposition **in** (*in, on*) = dative
>
> In **welcher** Straße wohnt er?

> **What** *film are you talking about?*
>
>> Restructured: *about what* film are you talking
>> Gender: **Der Film** (*film*) is masculine.
>> Number: singular
>> Case: Object of preposition **von** (*about*) = dative
>
> Von **welchem** Film sprecht ihr?

NOTE: The word *what* is not always an interrogative adjective. In the sentence "*What* is on the table?" it is an interrogative pronoun; in German you would ask "**Was** ist auf dem Tisch?" (See **What is an Interrogative Pronoun?**, p. 147.)

Practice

I. In the following sentences:
  • Underline the interrogative adjective.
  • Circle the noun about which a question is being asked.

1. What newspaper do you read?

2. Which record did you buy?

3. Do you know what homework is due?

4. Which hotel are you staying at?

5. Which game did you see?

II. Rewrite these questions in English to eliminate the dangling prepositions.

1. Which topic did you write about?

_____

2. Which people did you talk to?

_____

What is an Adverb?

An **adverb** is a word that describes a verb, an adjective, or another adverb. Adverbs indicate quantity, time, place, intensity, and manner.

Kathy drives *well.*
|
verb

The house is *very* big.
|
adjective

The girl ran *too* quickly.
|
adverb

In English: Here are some examples of adverbs:

- of quantity or degree

    Mary sleeps *little.*
    Bob does *well enough* in class.

    These adverbs answer the question *how much?* or *how well?*

- of time

    He will come *soon.*
    The children arrived *late.*

    These adverbs answer the question *when?*

- of place

    The teacher looked *around.*
    The old were left *behind.*

    These adverbs answer the question *where?*

- of intensity

> The roses are *really* beautiful.
> Gail can *actually* read Latin.

These adverbs are used for *emphasis.*

- of manner

> Mark sings *beautifully.*
> They parked the car *carefully.*

These adverbs answer the question *how?* They are the most common adverbs and can usually be recognized by their -ly ending.

A few adverbs in English are identical in form to the corresponding adjectives:

The guests came *late.* adverb	We greeted the *late* guests. adjective
Don't drive so *fast.* adverb	*Fast* drivers cause accidents. adjective
She works very *hard.* adverb	This is *hard* work. adjective

NOTE: Remember that in English *good* is an adjective; *well* is an adverb.

> That student writes *good* essays.
>
> *Good* modifies the noun *essays;* it is an adjective.
>
> That student writes *well.*
>
> *Well* modifies the verb *writes;* it is an adverb.

In German: German adverbs have the same form as their corresponding adjectives. They are like the small group of English adverb-adjectives above.

ADVERB	ADJECTIVE
Wir fahren **schnell**.	Der Wagen ist **schnell**.
We drive fast.	*The car is fast.*
Sie singen **schön**.	Das Lied ist **schön**.
They sing beautifully.	*The song is beautiful.*
Du hast das **gut** gemacht.	Dieses Buch ist **gut**.
You did that well.	*This book is good.*

As in English, there are also words that can function only as adverbs.

Das Haus ist **sehr** groß.
*The house is **very** big.*

Er kommt **bald**.
*He is coming **soon**.*

Practice

In the following sentences:
- Circle the adverbs.
- Draw an arrow from each adverb to the word it modifies in the space provided above each sentence.

1. The guests arrived early.

2. They were too tired to go out.

3. David learned the lesson really quickly.

4. We stayed here.

5. Meg is a good student who speaks German very well.

What is a Preposition?

A **preposition** is a word that shows the relationship of one word (usually a noun or pronoun) to another word in the sentence. Prepositions normally indicate position, direction, time, or manner.

In English: Here are some examples of prepositions showing:

- position

    They are *in* the car.
    She is sitting *behind* you.

- direction
    We went *to* school.
    The students came directly *from* class.

- time
    Many Germans vacation *in* August.
    Their son will be home *at* Christmas.

- manner
    They left *without* us.
    He writes *with* a pen.

The noun or pronoun which the preposition connects to the rest of the sentence is called the **object of the preposition**. The preposition and its object together make up a **prepositional phrase**.

In German: As in English, prepositions are invariable, i.e., they never change form. However, the object of the preposition can be in the accusative, dative, or genitive case, depending on the preposition. For this reason, as you memorize each German preposition, you must memorize the case that follows it. Below are examples of the various cases that prepositions take.

2. If the agent of a passive sentence is a person, it is expressed by **von** + dative object:

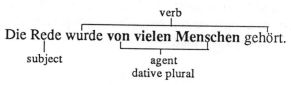

The speech was heard by many people.

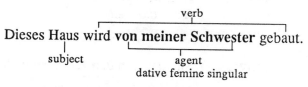

This house is being built by my sister.

3. If the agent is not a person, it is usually expressed by **durch** + accusative object:

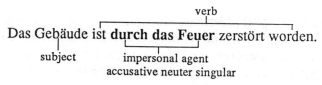

The building was destroyed by the fire.

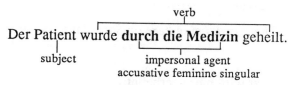

The patient was healed by the medicine.

4. If you change a sentence that has only a dative object from active to passive, the dative object does not become the nominative subject of the new sentence. Instead, it remains in the dative case. Since these passive sentences have no grammatical subject, the verb is always singular.

ACTIVE: Man dankt **ihm.**
                subject verb dative object

                *One thanks **him.***

PASSIVE: **Ihm** wird gedankt.
                ***He** is thanked.*

ACTIVE: Sie glaubten **den Kindern** nicht.
                subject verb   dative object

                *They didn't believe **the children.***

PASSIVE: **Den Kindern** wurde nicht geglaubt.
                ***The children** were not believed.*

Unlike English, German sometimes uses intransitive verbs (verbs that cannot have a direct object) in the passive voice. In this usage, these verbs express activity as such, and there is no agent. Such constructions are called **impersonal passives**, and they cannot be translated adequately into English.

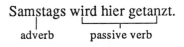

Samstags wird hier getanzt.
  adverb   passive verb

There is dancing here on Saturdays.

Jetzt wird hier gearbeitet.
  adverb   passive verb

Work is being done here now.

These German sentences have no grammatical subject.

Your textbook will show you several alternatives to the passive construction in German.

Practice

I. In the following sentences:
- Underline the subject of the sentence.
- Place a check by the performer of the action.
- Identify each sentence by writing "A" for active or "P" for passive on the line.

1. The cow jumped over the moon. _____

2. The game was cut short by rain. _____

3. They camped by the river. _____

4. We were awakened by a loud noise. _____

5. This film will be enjoyed by everyone. _____

II. The sentences below are in active voice.
- Underline the verb.
- Identify the tense on the line at the end of the sentence.
- Rewrite the sentence in the passive voice on the line below, keeping the same tense.

1. The parents dropped off the children.

_____

2. Work crews are clearing the road.

_____

3. People all over the world will see this program.

_____

What is a Conjunction?

A **conjunction** is a word that links words or groups of words.

In English: There are two kinds of conjunctions: coordinating and subordinating.

1. **Coordinating conjunctions** join words, phrases, and clauses that are equal; they *coordinate* elements of equal rank. The major coordinating conjunctions in English are *and, but, or, nor,* and *for.*

   > good *or* evil
   > over the river *and* through the woods
   > They invited us, *but* we couldn't come.

2. **Subordinating conjunctions** join a dependent clause to the main clause; they *subordinate* one thought to another one; that is, they indicate the relationship of unequal elements. A clause introduced by a subordinating conjunction is called a dependent or subordinate clause. (See p. 221.) Typical subordinating conjunctions are *although, because, if, unless, so that, while, that,* and *whatever.*

   > *Although* we were invited, we didn't go.
   >   subordinating conjunction   main clause
   >
   > They left *because* they were bored.
   > main clause   subordinating conjunction
   >
   > He said *that* he was tired.
   > main clause   subordinating conjunction

Notice that the main clause is not always the first clause of the sentence.

Some words function as both prepositions and subordinating conjunctions.

PREPOSITION OR SUBORDINATING CONJUNCTION

We can decide whether a word is a preposition or a subordinating conjunction by determining whether it introduces a clause.

If it introduces a clause, the word is a subordinating conjunction. The clause will contain a subject and a verb (see **What are Sentences, Phrases, and Clauses?**, p. 216).

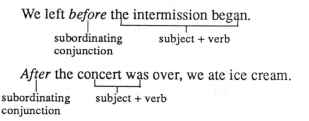

We left *before* the intermission began.
       subordinating   subject + verb
       conjunction

After the concert was over, we ate ice cream.
  subordinating   subject + verb
  conjunction

If the word in question does not introduce a clause, it is a preposition. The prepositional phrase contains an object, but no verb.

We left *before* the intermission.
    preposition   object of preposition

After the concert we ate ice cream.
 preposition   object of preposition

In German: Conjunctions are to be memorized as vocabulary items. Like adverbs and prepositions, conjunctions are invariable (i.e., they never change their form), but they do have their own rules of usage. Your German textbook will explain these special rules.

The major coordinating conjunctions are **und** (*and*), **oder** (*or*), **aber** (*but*), **sondern** (*but = on the contrary*), and **denn** (*for*). Typical subordinating conjunctions include **obgleich** (*although*), **obwohl** (*although*), **weil** (*because*), **wenn** (*if, whenever*), **damit** (*in order that*), **daß** (*that*), and **während** (*while*).

It is important for you to distinguish between prepositions and conjunctions in German, because you will use different words and apply different rules of grammar depending on which part of speech you use. In English it is easy to overlook the part of speech to which a word belongs because we sometimes use the same word as a preposition and as a conjunction.

ENGLISH	GERMAN	
PREPOSITION	PREPOSITION	CONJUNCTION
CONJUNCTION		
before	vor	bevor
after	nach	nachdem

Let us look at some examples using these different parts of speech.

> *We left **before** the intermission.*
> | |
> preposition   object of preposition

> Wir sind **vor** der Pause weggegangen.

> *We left **before** the intermission began.*
> | |_____|
> subordinating   subject + verb
> conjunction

> Wir sind weggegangen, **bevor** die Pause anfing.

> ***After** the concert we ate ice cream.*
> | |
> preposition   object of preposition

> **Nach** dem Konzert haben wir Eis gegessen.

> ***After** the concert was over, we ate ice cream.*
> | |_____|
> subordinating   subject + verb
> conjunction

> **Nachdem** das Konzert vorbei war, aßen wir Eis.

To make sure you use the proper word in German and apply the proper rules of grammar, you must learn the part of speech of each vocabulary word you memorize.

Practice

I. In the following sentences:
   - Circle the coordinating and subordinating conjunctions.
   - Underline the words each conjunction serves to coordinate or to subordinate with the main part of the sentence.

1. We can have a picnic unless it starts raining.

2. She stopped studying because she was too tired.

3. He forgot his watch, but he remembered his passport.

4. They saved money so they could visit Austria.

5. After school let's go home and have a snack.

II. The sentences below contain prepositions and conjunctions.
   - Underline the prepositions.
   - Box in the conjunctions.

1. Since the weather turned cold, we'll stayed inside.

2. I've know him since high school.

3. We were home before midnight.

4. Before we leave, we'd better say goodbye.

5. After you pick up your room, you can go out.

What are Sentences, Phrases, and Clauses?

WHAT IS A SENTENCE?

A **sentence** is a group of words that act together as a complete unit. Typically a sentence consists of at least a subject (see **What is a Subject?**, p. 30) and a verb (see **What is a Verb?**, p. 26).

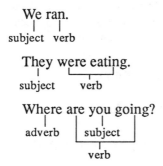

We ran.
subject verb

They were eating.
subject   verb

Where are you going?
adverb   subject
         verb

Depending on the verb, a sentence may also have direct and indirect objects (see **What are Objects?**, p. 33).

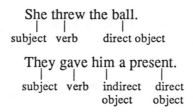

She threw the ball.
subject verb   direct object

They gave him a present.
subject verb indirect direct
             object   object

In addition, a sentence may include various kinds of modifiers: adjectives (see **What is an Adjective?**, p. 169), adverbs (see **What is an Adverb?**, p. 189), prepositional phrases (see **What is a Preposition?**, p. 192), participial phrases (see **What is a Participle?**, p. 98).

I saw a movie.
subject verb   object

I saw a *great* movie.
adjective

Yesterday I saw a great movie.
 |
 adverb

Yesterday *after work* I saw a great movie.
 └─────┬─────┘
 prepositional phrase modifying *saw*

Attracted by the reviews, I saw a great movie yesterday.
└──────────┬──────────┘
 participial phrase modifying *I*

Although not all these elements occur in a German sentence in the same way that they do in English, you will find it very helpful to recognize the different parts of a sentence in each language. Moreover, it will be important for you to recognize complete sentences and to distinguish phrases and clauses from complete sentences.

WHAT IS A PHRASE?

A **phrase** is simply a group of words that belong together on the basis of their meaning. We identify phrases by the type of word that introduces them.

Prepositional phrase—begins with a preposition

        through the door
         | |
   preposition   object of preposition

        after the concert
        | |
   preposition   object of preposition

Participial phrase—begins with a participle

        leaving the room
        | |
  present participle   object of *leaving*
    of *to leave*

        pasted on the wall
        | |
  past participle   prepositional phrase used
    of *to paste*   adverbially to modify *pasted*

Infinitive phrase—begins with an infinitive

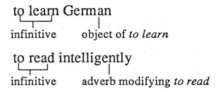

To recognize such phrases you need to find the individual parts (prepositions, participles, infinitives) and notice how the group of words works as one block of meaning.

WHAT IS A CLAUSE?

A **clause** is a group of words that contains its own subject and conjugated verb.

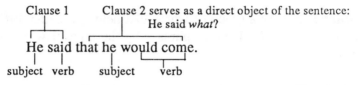

You can distinguish these clauses from a phrase by the presence of a subject and a conjugated verb in each one (see p. 209). You can see that they are different from a complete sentence if you try to use them separately. Neither "he said" nor "that he would come" expresses a finished thought; therefore neither is a complete sentence. Instead, both are parts of a whole sentence.

WHAT ARE THE VARIOUS TYPES OF SENTENCES?

A. A **simple sentence** is a sentence consisting of only one clause.

In English: There is no set position for the verb in an English sentence or clause, but the subject almost always comes before the verb.

> We went to the concert.
> | |
> subject verb

A modifier can also come before the subject.

> Yesterday we went to a concert.
> |
> adverb

> After the party we went to a concert.
> L_____T_____J
> prepositional phrase modifying *went*

In German: In a simple declarative sentence (a statement), the conjugated verb always stands in second position. This does not mean that the verb is always the second word in the sentence; it means that if the sentence begins with some modifier, for example, an adverb or a prepositional phrase, the verb follows immediately. Compare the structure of these German sentences with that of their literal English translations:

> Wir **gingen** in ein Konzert.
> | |
> subject   verb
> 1st   2nd
> position position

> *we **went** to a concert*

> Gestern **gingen** wir in ein Konzert.
> | | |
> adverb   verb subject
> 1st   2nd
> position   position

> *yesterday **went** we to a concert*

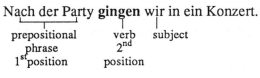

Nach der Party **gingen** wir in ein Konzert.

prepositional phrase 1stposition	verb 2nd position	subject

*after the party **went** we to a concert*

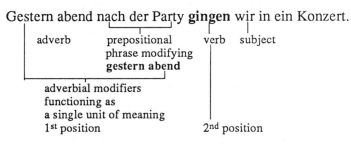

Gestern abend nach der Party **gingen** wir in ein Konzert.

adverb	prepositional phrase modifying **gestern abend**	verb	subject

adverbial modifiers functioning as a single unit of meaning
1st position   2nd position

*yesterday evening after the party **went** we to a concert*

Only in the first example is it possible to put the subject before the verb in the German sentence. In the other sentences that space is already occupied by a modifier; the verb must come second, and the subject must follow the verb.

B. A **compound sentence** consists of two equal clauses. These two statements are joined by coordinating conjunctions (see **What is a Conjunction?**, p. 212). In both English and German the word order is the same as for any simple sentence.

In English: The position of the verb can vary in a simple sentence, though the subject usually comes before the verb.

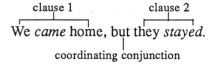

clause 1   clause 2
We *came* home, but they *stayed*.
coordinating conjunction

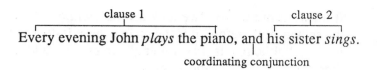

clause 1   clause 2

Every evening John *plays* the piano, and his sister *sings*.

coordinating conjunction

In German: It is important that you know how to recognize a compound sentence. Usually the two statements of a compound sentence are both simple sentences. This means that in German each of them will have the conjugated verb in second position:

> *We came home, but they stayed.*
> Wir sind nach Hause gekommen, aber sie sind geblieben.
>
> subject verb   conjunction subject verb
> 1st   2nd   1st   2nd
> position position   position position

> *Meg sings and every evening John plays the piano.*
> Meg singt und jeden Abend spielt John Klavier.
>
> subject verb conjunction adverb verb subject object
> 1st   2nd   1st   2nd
> position position   position position

The coordinating conjunction between the two clauses has no effect on the word order of the second clause.

C. A **complex sentence** is a sentence consisting of a main clause and one or more dependent clauses:

The **main clause** (or independent clause) in a complex sentence could stand alone as a complete sentence.

The **dependent clause** (including relative clauses) cannot stand alone as a complete sentence; it depends on the main clause for its full meaning, and it is subordinate to the main clause.

> dependent clause   main clause
> Although it was raining, we took a walk.

It makes sense to say "we took a walk" without the first clause in the sentence; therefore, it is the main clause. It does not make sense to say, "although it was raining" unless we add a conclusion; therefore, it is the dependent clause.

In English: It is important that you be able to distinguish a main clause from a dependent clause. This will help you to write complete sentences and avoid sentence fragments.

In German: It is important for you to learn to distinguish between the main clause and the dependent clause in German, because each type of clause has its own word order.

In the main clause the verb remains in the same position as in the simple sentence; that is, the verb will be in second position in a German sentence, unlike in English where the position may vary.

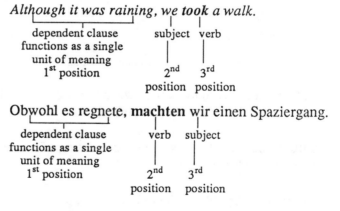

Although it was raining, we took a walk.

dependent clause
functions as a single
unit of meaning
1st position   subject   verb
     2nd   3rd
     position position

Obwohl es regnete, **machten** wir einen Spaziergang.

dependent clause
functions as a single
unit of meaning
1st position   verb   subject
     2nd   3rd
     position position

In dependent clauses, including both clauses introduced by subordinating conjunctions and relative clauses, the conjugated verb stands at the end, except in a few special constructions.

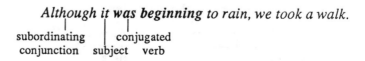

Although it was beginning to rain, we took a walk.

subordinating   conjugated
conjunction   subject   verb

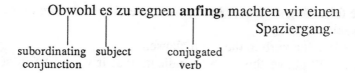

Obwohl es zu regnen **anfing,** machten wir einen
Spaziergang.

subordinating   subject   conjugated
conjunction   verb

Your German textbook will explain this structure in more detail.
The important point is that you be able to recognize a dependent
clause when you see one.

Practice

I. Underline the phrases in these sentences.

1. It is important to do your best.

2. Before the play we ate out.

3. Chris remembered the appointment at the last minute.

4. They wanted to start early in the morning.

5. Jane spent an hour organizing her room.

II. Box in the dependent clauses in these sentences.

1. While you were out, someone called.

2. Although we were tired, we had fun.

3. They said that they were ready.

4. Let us know if you want to go with us.

5. After the sun set, the park closed for the day.

III. The following sentences in English have different word order from German sentences.
  - Underline the verb in the main clause.
  - Write "2" above this verb to indicate that it would be in second position in a German sentence.

1. Last night it snowed.

2. They really looked surprised.

3. With computers the work goes faster.

4. Tomorrow I have an appointment.

5. By the time we arrived, things were over.

Appendix—Selected Noun Gender Reference List

1. MASCULINE (maskulin)

- Nouns referring to masculine persons which end in **-er, -ist, -ling, -ent**. Plural formed by adding **—, -e,** or **-en.**

der Physiker	die Physiker
der Jüngling	die Jünglinge
der Pianist	die Pianisten
der Referent	die Referenten

A more general rule: nouns referring to human beings are masculine unless they specifically refer to females (which then have feminine gender). Be careful, however, with diminutives (**das Fräulein, das Mädchen**), which are discussed below.

- Names of seasons, months, days, parts of days (except **die Nacht**), geographical directions, and weather phenomenona

> der Sommer
> der Januar
> der Montag
> der Mittag
> der Wind
> der West

NOTE: **das Frühjahr,** another terms for **der Frühling,** is neuter because **Jahr** is neuter.

- Most nouns which end in:

-ig	der Pfennig
-or	der Motor, der Doktor
-ismus	der Optimismus

2. FEMININE **(feminin)**

- Most 2-syllable nouns which end in **-e**. Plural formed by adding **-n**.

die Lampe	die Lampen
die Seife	die Seifen

  (Some common exceptions are: **der Name, der Käse, das Auge.**)

- Nouns referring to female human beings which end in **-in**. Plural formed by adding **-nen**.

die Studentin	die Studentinnen
die Professorin	die Professorinnen

- Nouns which end in:

-ei	die Bücherei	die Büchereien
-ie	die Drogerie	die Drogerien
-heit	die Dummheit	die Dummheiten
-keit	die Möglichkeit	die Möglichkeiten
-schaft	die Mannschaft	die Mannschaften
-ung	die Prüfung	die Prüfungen
-ion	die Reaktion	die Reaktionen
-tät	die Universität	die Universitäten
-ade	die Fassade	die Fassaden
-ik	die Musik	
-ur	die Natur	
-unft	die Vernunft	
-enz	die Lizenz	die Lizenzen

3. NEUTER **(neutral)**

- Nouns ending in the diminutives suffixes **-lein** or **-chen**. Plural just like singular.

das Mädchen	die Mädchen
das Büchlein	die Büchlein
das Fräulein	die Fräulein

- Verb infinitives used as nouns (gerunds). No plural possible.

  das Lesen
  das Essen
  das Singen

- The names of most cities, continents, and countries.

  (das) Berlin
  (das) Europa
  (das) Deutschland

NOTE: Unless preceded by an adjective, articles are not usually used with these nouns. There are important exceptions as well, masculine and feminine place names that do take articles, for example:

  die Antarktis
  die Bundesrepublik Deutschland
  die Deutsche Demokratische Republik
  der Libanon
  die Schweiz

- Most nouns which end in **-um**. Plural with $\ddot{}$**-er.**

  das Bistum   die Bistümer

Answer Key

What is a Noun?
1. student, teacher, question 2. textbook, picture, cover 3. children, room 4. Eric, tape deck, birthday 5. cows, middle, field 6. actions, words 7. parents, Berlin, year 8. honesty, policy 9. audience, wit, candor 10. teacher, explanations, class

What is Meant by Gender?
I. 1. ? 2. feminine 3. masculine 4. ? 5. ?
II. 1. masculine 2. neuter 3. feminine 4. masculine 5. feminine

What is Meant by Number?
I. 1. plural 2. singular 3. singular 4. plural 5. singular
II. 1. ö + -er 2. ü + -e 3. -er 4. -en 5. -s

What are Articles?
I. 1. das 2. die 3. der 4. die 5. das II. 1. the 2. a 3. the 4. a 5. the

What is Meant by Case?
I. 1. the children, the ball 2. the cat, the mice 3. a car, the drive 4. an insider, the story, the press 5. the end, the movie, a surprise
II. Fill in left to right: nominative; direct object; dative; possessive; object of a preposition

What is a Verb?
1. eat 2. met 3. stayed, expected 4. took, finished, went 5. felt, talked

What is a Subject?
1. Q: What leaves? A: The bus. 2. Q: What was over? Who went home? A: The game. Everyone. 3. Q: Who checked the books out? A: Emily. 4. Q: Who could see the solution? A: Stefan. 5. Q: Who took a boat ride? A: My friends and I.

What are Objects?
1. Q: What did the computer lose? A: My homework. DO
2. Q: What did she borrow? A: The car. DO 3. Q: About what are you worried? A: About the test. OP 4. Q: What did he send? To whom did he send it? A: A postcard. To his friend. DO + IO 5. Q: For what did they pay? With what did they pay? A: The books. A credit card. OP + OP

What is a Predicate Noun?
The subject is after the comma: 1. news, letter 2. doctor, Carol
3. tourists, they 4. musician, Dan 5. place, pool

What is the Possessive?
The possessor is in *italics*: 1. the motor of the *car* 2. the results of a *test* 3. the end of the *year* 4. the tale of two *cities* 5. the works of *Schiller*

What is a Pronoun?
The antecedent is after the comma: 1. she, Brooke 2. they, Molly and Stan 3. it, chair 4. himself, Jim 5. her, Helga

What is a Personal Pronoun?
I. 1. I, **ich** 2. they, **sie** 3. you, **du** (familiar)/**Sie** (formal) 4. we, **wir**
5. you, **ihr** (familiar)/**Sie** (formal) 6. he, she, it, **er, sie, es** II. 1. du
2. wir 3. ihr 4. sie 5. Sie III. 1. it, **es** 2. it, **sie** 3. it, **er**
IV. Nouns referring to persons are in *italics*: 1. *Greg*, preposition + pronoun 2. present, da-compound 3. *Emily*, preposition + pronoun
4. vacation, da-compound 5. weather, da-compound
V. 1. 2nd person, singular, dative 2. 3rd person, singular, dative, feminine 3. 1st person, singular, accusative 4. 3rd person, singular, accusative, masculine 5. 1st person, singular, dative

What are the Principal Parts of a Verb?
I. Fill in left to right: 1. opened 2. came 3. washed 4. drunk 5. to fall II. 1. weak 2. strong 3. strong 4. weak 5. strong

What is an Infinitive?
1. teach 2. be 3. have 4. leave 5. swim

What is a Verb Conjugation?
I. 1. denk- 2. renn- 3. arbeit- 4. wander- 5. reis- II. -e, -st, -t, -en,
-t, -en III. Stem: geh-; gehe, gehst, geht, gehen, geht, gehen
IV. 1. Matt and I, **wir** 2. you (Karen and Doug), **ihr** 3. you (Prof.
Seidler), **Sie** 4. strawberries and peaches, **sie** 5. Ann and Bob, **sie**

What is the Present Tense?
1. do play, **spielen** 2. plays, **spielt** 3. is playing, **spielt**
4. are playing, **spielen** 5. do play, **spielst**

What is the Past Tense?
I. 1. wrote, was writing, did write 2. laughed, was laughing, did
laugh II. 1. spoke 2. rained 3. telephoned

What are Auxiliary Verbs?
I. 1. are 2. can 3. do 4. has been 5. will II. Verbs to be under-
lined are in *italics*. 1. is coming 2. *reads* 3. *drives* 4. are packing
5. does have

What is a Participle?
I. 1. working; present 2. spilled; past 3. falling; present 4. singing;
present 5. sunken; past 6. heated; past 7. basking; present
II. Gerunds are in *italics*: 1. flying, driving 2. *coming* 3. littering
4. sunbathing 5. *turning*

What are the Perfect Tenses?
1. had said (-2), climbed (-1) 2. wants (0), called (-1) 3. saw (-1),
had read (-2) 4. asked (-1), had seen (-2) 5. had finished (-2), went
(-1)

What is the Future Tense?
1. are going, present 2. is, future of probability 3. shall return, future 4. will tell, future 5. 'll be, future 6. cost, future of probability
7. are leaving, present 8. will climb, future 9. gets, present
10. come, future of probability

What is Meant by Mood?
1. indicative 2. subjunctive 3. imperative 4. indicative
5. indicative 6. subjunctive 7. imperative

What is the Imperative?
1. du 2. wir 3. ihr 4. Sie 5. du

What is the Subjunctive?
I. 1. F 2. CTF 3. CTF 4. F 5. CTF II. 1. were, present
2. would do, present; had, present 3. had planned, past; would have
packed, past 4. would like, present 5. were, present; would wear,
present 6. had called, past; would have come, past 7. had stopped,
past III. Subjunctive verbs are in *italics:* 1. wish, *were* 2. *would
comment* 3. *knew*, are missing 4. *would like*, don't have 5. *would
have been, had been tied up*

What is Meant by Direct and Indirect Discourse?
I. 1. is, present, . . .how the weather was 2. found, past, we, . . .they
had found the trail 3. got, past, I/my, . . .he had just gotten his
driver's license 4. 'm coming, present, I, . . .she was coming
5. 'm done, present, I, . . .he was done II. 1. was studying, she,
"I am studying." 2. had ratified, "The Senate has ratified the
treaty." 3. was, he, "I am tired." 4. had been lost, they, "We were
lost." 5. had hidden, she/her, "I hid my toy."

What is a Possessive Pronoun?
1. yours 2. ours 3. hers 4. his 5. mine

What is a Reflexive Pronoun?
1. yourself 2. ourselves 3. himself 4. herself 5. myself
6. yourselves

What is a Reflexive Verb?
mich, dich, sich, uns, euch, sich

What is an Interrogative Pronoun?
1. who, subject, person, **wer** 2. what, direct object, thing, **was**
3. whose, possessive, person (or thing), **wessen** 4. who(m),
direct object, person, **wen** 5. who (for whom), object of preposition,
person, **wen**

What is a Relative Pronoun?
The antecedent is in *italics*: I. 1. that, *letter*, DO 2. who, *people*, S
3. whom, *woman*, DO 4. whose, *book*, PM 5. whom, *student*, OP
II. 1. dog/it, *dog*, it, subject, that (which), The dog that lives next
door is friendly. 2. Smiths/them, *Smiths*, them, direct object, who(m),
The Smiths, who(m) you met in Basel, left for Austria. 3. stu-
dent/her, *student*, her, object of preposition, who(m), The new student,
about whom you were asking, is German./The new student you were
asking about is German.

What is a Descriptive Adjective?
I. The noun or pronoun described is after the comma: 1. old, dog;
new, tricks 2. tired, we; long, walk 3. excellent, meal 4. dark,
clouds; high, mountains 5. popular, sports   II. Predicate adjectives
are in *italics*: 1. *fresh*; red, green 2. *expensive*; new 3. *tired*;
younger 4. *impressive*; old 5. *hard to find*; good

What is Meant by Comparison of Adjectives?
I. 1. The teacher is older than the students. 2. This student is as
intelligent as that one. 3. Kathy is less tall than Molly.
4. This movie is the best this season. 5. Today is the hottest day on
record. II. 1. AA 2. PA 3. PA 4. AA 5. AA

What is a Possessive Adjective?
I. The possessive adjective is in *italics*: 1. *their* exams 2. *her* coat,
her scarf 3. *his* comb, *his* pocket 4. *her* brother 5. *his* sister
II. 1. my, key, singular, accusative, **mein + -en** 2. your, aunt,
feminine, singular, **dein + -er**

What is an Interrogative Adjective?

I. The interrogative adjective is in *italics*: 1. *what* newspaper
2. *which* record 3. *what* homework 4. *which* hotel 5. *which* game
II. 1. About which topic did you write? 2. To which people did you talk?

What is an Adverb?

The word modified is after the comma: 1. early, arrived 2. too, tired
3. really, quickly, learned 4. here, stayed 5. very, well, speaks

What is a Preposition?

I. 1. behind 2. under 3. in, in 4. on, around   II. 1. I can't tell about what they're laughing. 2. About what is she excited? 3. For whom are you doing that?

What are Prefixes and Suffixes?

I. 1. de- 2. en- 3. mis- 4. re- 5. un-   II. 1. -ency 2. -ful
3. -less 4. -en 5. -er III. 1. die 2. der 3. das 4. die 5. die
IV. 1. s 2. is 3. is 4. s 5. s

What is Meant by Active and Passive Voice?

I. The performer of the action is in *italics*: 1. cow, *cow*, A 2. game, *rain*, P 3. they, *they*, A 4. we, *noise*, P 5. film, *everyone*, P
II. 1. dropped, past, The children were dropped off by the parents.
2. are clearing, present, The road is being cleared by work crews.
3. will see, future, This program will be seen by people all over the world.

What is a Conjunction?

The conjunctions are in italics: I. 1. *unless*, it starts raining
2. *because*, she was too tired 3. *but*, he remembered his passport
4. *so*, they could visit Austria 5. *and*, have a snack   II. 1. *since*
2. since 3. *before* 4. before 5. *after*

What are Sentences, Phrases, and Clauses?

I. 1. *to do your best* 2. *Before the play* 3. *at the last minute* 4. *to start early, in the morning* 5. *organizing her room*   II. 1. While you were out 2. Although we were tired 3. that they were ready
4. if you want to go with us 5. After the sun set   III. 1. snowed
2. looked 3. goes 4. have 5. were

Index

a, an 14-15
    see also indefinite article
accusative 23, 24, 35, 38, 56, 208
    object of preposition 38, 193-194
    of interrogative pronoun 150, 152
    of personal pronoun 57
    of reflexive pronoun 137
    w/ preposition 39
active voice 204-211
adjective 98-100, 169-170
    attributive 99, 100, 104, 106,
        170-174, 179
    comparative 171-181
    demonstrative 169
    descriptive 165, 170-174
    interrogative 169, 181-188
    possessive 138, 165, 177-181
    predicate 170-171, 173-174
adjective endings 172-173
    strong 172
    weak 172
adverb 111, 115-116, 189-191
agent
    impersonal 209
    in passive voice 205-206
    personal agent 209
agreement 14, 31, 49, 115, 133,
    139, 182-183
antecedent 47, 49, 63
    indefinite 164-165
    of personal pronoun 54, 60-62,
        67, 68
    of relative pronoun 151-166
apostrophe 43
article 14-18
    see also definite article and
    indefinite article

attributive adjective 99, 100, 104,
    106, 170-174, 179
    in comparative degree 175-176,
        177-178
    in superlative degree 175-180
auxiliary verb 88, 92-99, 109, 205

be 93, 95
    in passive voice 104, 205
    in subjunctive 123, 125

case 15, 18-26, 31, 38, 170, 172,
    182, 186, 208
    of interrogative pronoun 148-153
    of personal pronoun 49-51, 56-57,
        61, 63
    of reflexive pronoun 133
    of relative pronoun 161-164
class 2
clause 218
    dependent 155-156, 221-223
    relative 155
    subordinate 155, 212-209
cognate 1
collective noun 12
command 119-121
common noun 5
compound noun 5
compound tense 91, 98
conditional 124, 130
conjugated verb 31, 78, 219-221
conjugation 79-87
conjunction 212-215
    co-ordinating 212-213, 221
    subordinating 212-214
contrary-to-fact condition 122,
    124, 128

da-compound 64, 68
dative 23-24, 35-37, 56
   in passive sentence 210
   object of verb 35-37, 65
   of interrogative pronoun 150-152
   of personal pronoun 57
   of reflexive pronoun 137
   with preposition 38, 45, 193-194,
     205
declension 14-16, 22, 23, 24, 161,
   172, 186
demonstrative adjective 169
descriptive adjective 165, 170-174
direct discourse 132-133
direct object
   see object, direct
do, does 93-95

extended adjectival construction
   100, 106-107

familiar you 52-53, 57-58, 66,
   81-82
feminine 7-9, 16-17, 45, 54, 61, 200
finite verb 77
first person 50-51, 81-82, 133
formal you 53, 57-59, 66, 82-83
function 3-4, 15, 18, 23-25, 50, 57,
   59-60, 149, 156, 160, 162
future of probability 116
future perfect tense 73, 110,
   112-113
future tense 73, 87, 94, 114-117

ge- prefix 75, 104-105
gender 7-10, 24, 49, 53-54, 133,
   170, 172, 182, 186, 225-227
genitive 23-24, 44-45, 56, 153,
   193-194
gerund 101-103, 223

haben 93, 106, 110-113, 127, 134
have 93, 103-104, 109-110
he 47, 50-51, 56, 67
helping verb 88, 92-97
   see also **haben, sein, werden**
her 3, 21, 55-57, 60, 67, 181-182
hers 136-137
herself 48, 139, 141
him 55-57, 59, 67
himself 139, 141
his 136-137, 181-182

I 19, 47, 50-51, 56, 65, 81
idiom 2
if-clause 124, 128
imperative 118-121
imperfect tense
   see simple past
impersonal passive 210
indefinite antecedents 164-165
indefinite articles 14, 16, 21, 172,
   179
indicative 118-119, 120, 122, 123,
   125
indirect discourse subjunctive 132-136
indirect object
   see object, indirect
infinitive 74-79, 96, 115, 125, 127,
   141, 201, 218
-ing
   gerund 101-102
   participle 98-99
inseparable prefix 201-202
interrogative adjective 169,
   181-188
interrogative pronoun 48, 147-155
intransitive verb 27-28, 210
irregular verb 74, 103
it 48, 50-51, 53-54, 57, 60, 67-68
its 136, 181-182
itself 139, 141

let's 120
linking verb 41-42, 170
-ly ending of adverb 190

main clause 221-222
main verb 78, 92-93, 109-110, 114
masculine 7-9, 15, 44, 54, 61
me 19, 48, 56-57, 65
meaning 1
mine 48, 136-137
modal auxiliary 95-96
mood 118-119
    imperative 118
    in indirect discourse 133
    indicative 118-119
    subjunctive 118-119, 122-132
my 181-182
myself 48, 139-142

necessity, expressions of 123, 125
neuter 7-8, 16, 44, 54, 61-62,
    199-200
nominative 20, 23, 31, 41-42, 208
of interrogative pronoun 147, 149
of personal pronoun 51, 56
non-restrictive clause 165-166
noun 4-6, 49, 54, 195-200, 225-227
    agreement with article 15
    collective 12
    used as adjective 5
    verbal noun 101-102, 223
    number 11-13, 24, 49, 137, 139,
        170, 172, 182, 186

object 27, 33-40, 55-64, 143,
    150-151, 153
    direct 20, 27, 33-36, 140-141,
        150-151, 153
    indirect 20, 33-37, 140-141, 151,
        158

of preposition 20, 33, 37-38, 62-64,
    102, 141, 143, 147, 152,
    158-159, 187, 192-194
objective 20-21, 55-56, 143, 147
of 43
our 181-182
ours 137
ourselves 139, 141

part of speech 2, 3, 4, 199
participial phrase 99, 104, 217
participle 95, 98-108, 217
    past 73, 98, 103-107, 134
    present 95, 98-103
passive voice 93-94, 106, 204-211
past emphatic 90
past participle 73-76, 98, 103-107,
    134, 207
past perfect 73, 90, 110-111
    see also pluperfect
past progressive 90
past subjunctive 127-128
past tense 73-76, 87, 90-92
    past emphatic 90
    past progressive 90
    simple past 73, 90-92, 123, 125
perfect tense 90-91, 93, 109-114,
    207
personal endings 84
personal pronoun 47, 50-73, 141
    flow charts 65-69
    in imperative 120-121
    as object 47-48, 55-62
    as object of preposition 48, 62-63
    as subject 47, 50-54
phrase 216-224
    participial 99, 217
    prepositional 192, 217
    infinitive 218
pluperfect 110-112, 207

plural 11-12, 45, 50-53, 82-83,
   225-227
Plusquamperfekt
   see pluperfect 110-112
possessive 21, 43-46, 148, 153, 159
possessive adjective 138, 165,
   177-181
possessive pronoun 21, 48, 136-138
predicate adjective 170-171,
   173-174
predicate noun 20-21, 23, 41-42
prefix 75, 104, 197-204
   inseparable 201-202
   separable 197, 200-201
preposition 37-39, 192-198,
   213-214
   dangling 151-152, 158-159, 183,
      196-197
   object of, *see* object of preposition
   two-way 194
prepositional phrase 192, 217
present participle 95, 98-103
present perfect 90, 109
present subjunctive 123-127
present tense 73, 79-85, 87-89,
   115-116, 120
   emphatic 88
   perfect 109-114
   progressive 88
preterite tense
   see simple past
principal parts 73-77
pronominal adverb 64
pronoun 19-21, 47-49, 133
   direct object 47, 56-62
   indirect object 48, 56-62
   interrogative 48, 147-155
   object 20-21, 47-48
   object of preposition 48, 56, 62-64,
      139, 141, 158-159
   possessive 21, 48, 136-138

reflexive 48, 139-144
relative 48, 155-168
subject 20, 47, 50-54, 79-83, 120,
   121, 139
proper noun 5, 43-45

reflexive pronoun 48, 139-144
reflexive verb 144-146
regular verb 74, 103
relative clause 151-166, 221
relative pronoun 48, 155-168
requests 125, 129
restrictive clause 165

second-person 50-53, 57-59, 76,
   81-83
sein 93, 106, 110-113, 127, 134
sentence 33, 216-224
   complete 27
   complex 221-223
   compound 220
   simple 218-221
separable prefix 197, 200-201
shall 114
she 47, 50-51, 56, 67
simple past 73, 90-92, 123, 125
simple tense 90
singular 11, 50-52
some 14
statement 215
stem of verb 84, 104-105, 126, 133
strong verbs 75, 85, 90, 104-105,
   202
subject 20-21, 23, 30, 32, 41-42,
   79-83, 139, 145, 156, 204, 216
subjunctive 118-119, 122-132
   general subjunctive 125-130, 133
   special subjunctive 133
   subjunctive I 133
   subjunctive II 125-130

subordinate clause 155, 209-212
suffix 75, 105, 198-204, 225-227

tense 87
that 2-3, 157
the 14, 22
   see also definite article
their 181-182
theirs 137
them 19-20, 47, 55-57, 69
themselves 139, 141
they 19-21, 47, 50-51, 56, 69, 83
third person 50-51, 53-54, 75-76,
   81-83

umlaut 12
us 20, 48, 55-57, 69
use 3

verb 26-30, 98-100
   auxiliary 88, 92-99, 109
   intransitive 28, 210
   irregular 103
   reflexive 144-146
   regular 74, 103
   transitive 27, 201
   strong 75, 85, 90, 104-105, 202
   weak 75, 90, 104-105, 202
   with prefixes 200-202
verbal noun 101-103
vocabulary 1
voice 204-205

we 20, 50-51, 56, 69, 82
   command 120-121

weak verbs 75, 90, 104-105, 202
werden 93-94, 106, 115, 127, 207
what 48
   interrogative adjective 185-187
   interrogative pronoun 148, 153, 187

which
   relative pronoun 157, 159
   interrogative pronoun 185-187
who
   interrogative pronoun 48, 147-152
   relative pronoun 48, 156
whom
   interrogative pronoun 147-152
   relative pronoun 157
whose
   interrogative pronoun 148-149, 153
   relative pronoun 48, 159
will 114
wishes 122, 124-125, 129
word order 18-19, 21, 115, 196,
   219-220, 222-223
would 124, 128, 130
would have 128
würde- construction 127, 130

you 50-51, 56, 81-83
   command 120-121
   familiar 52-53, 57-58, 66, 81-82
   formal 53, 57-59, 66, 82-83
your 181-182
yours 48, 136-137
yourself 139-143
yourselves 139, 141